Stress Management and Relaxation Techniques 2 in 1

Fast Proven Treatment for Stress & Anxiety

Nathan Golden

© **Copyright 2020 - All rights reserved.**

The content contained within this book may not be reproduced, duplicated or transmitted without direct written permission from the author or the publisher.

Under no circumstances will any blame or legal responsibility be held against the publisher, or author, for any damages, reparation, or monetary loss due to the information contained within this book, either directly or indirectly.

Legal Notice:

This book is copyright protected. It is only for personal use. You cannot amend, distribute, sell, use, quote or paraphrase any part, or the content within this book, without the consent of the author or publisher.

Disclaimer Notice:

Please note the information contained within this document is for educational and entertainment purposes only. All effort has been executed to present accurate, up to date, reliable, complete information. No warranties of any kind are declared or implied. Readers acknowledge that the author is not engaged in the rendering of legal, financial, medical or professional advice. The content within this book has been derived from various sources. Please consult a licensed professional before attempting any techniques outlined in this book.

By reading this document, the reader agrees that under no circumstances is the author responsible for any losses, direct or indirect, that are incurred as a result of the use of the information contained within this document, including, but not limited to, errors, omissions, or inaccuracies.

Table of Contents

Stress Management for the Beginners 5

Introduction 7

Chapter 1: Stressed? Join the Club and Get Started 12

Chapter 2: Do You Understand Stress? 28

Chapter 3: Managing Stress - The Basics 44

Chapter 4: Get Rid of Stress and Anxiety 58

Chapter 5: Relaxation Tips 74

Chapter 6: Calming Your Mind 88

Chapter 7: Organization and Time are Key 97

Chapter 8: Dealing with Stress in Real Life 109

Chapter 9: Seven Examples of Stressful Events - Explained 121

Chapter 10: The Seven Habits of Good Stress Managers - Explained 136

Conclusion 147

References 151

The Effective Relaxation Techniques **156**

Introduction 160

Chapter 1: The Secrets of Reacting to Stress and Anxiety 166

Chapter 2: General Tactics for Coping and Handling Stress 185

Chapter 3: The Basics of Relaxation Techniques .. 193

Chapter 4: The Examination Phase; Be Your Own Doctor 206

Chapter 5: Breathing Techniques Guide 222

Chapter 6: Body Scan Techniques Guide 243

Chapter 7: Progressive Relaxation Techniques Guide 258

Chapter 8: Physical Meditation Techniques Guide 272

Chapter 9: Visualization Techniques Guide 287

Chapter 10: Combine All the Techniques in Your Daily Routine 301

Final Thoughts 312

References 315

Stress Management for the Beginners

Stop Anxiety Now and Transform Your Life Through the Power of Stress Management

Nathan Golden

Free Stress Management Checklist!

(Ensure to take care of your well-being...)

This Checklist includes:

- Relaxation techniques you can do from home
- Stress Management timetable so you can organize your daily activities
- Progress monitorization log

The last thing we want is for your well-being to suffer because you weren't prepared.

To sign up and receive your survival checklist, click the link:

https://yourrelax53893.activehosted.com/f/1

We will send you an email shortly after you apply with details to download your checklist!

Introduction

You might be a parent caring for children. Maybe you're newly pregnant, or mired in a complex divorce. Perhaps you have just graduated from university and are wondering how you're ever going to pay off your student debt. Anxiety, heaviness in the chest, racing thoughts, and other symptoms of stress can be triggered by any major life event. Money, major changes, and complex problems can all be sources of chronic stress and anxiety.

If you feel like this is you, then you have come to the right place. In this book, I will provide you with all of the tools you need to manage stress, regardless of your life situation. This book will go over the basics of stress management, translating the psychological information into an easy, step-by-step guide that you can follow to bring your own stress and anxiety symptoms under control. By the end of this book, you will know exactly what causes your stress, and what steps you need to take to overcome it. The exercises in this book are here to get you started, but all of the strategies are designed to help you manage stress and anxiety in a sustainable way.

My name is Michael Robertson, and I have helped patients overcome their anxiety for years. During the course of my time as a professional, I have helped to transform the lives of hundreds of patients. My experience talking with people from all walks of life, who struggle to stop overthinking things and manage their anxiety, has given me a thorough understanding of how best to help people deal with these problems on a daily basis. Over time, I have developed an understanding of what works and what does not. Based on these observations of real people, I have seen how these strategies have impacted their lives and what strategies seem to work more often than others. But these techniques are not only for my patients' use - I have also taught them to my family, my friends, and I still use many myself. I can tell you from my own lived experience that this book will improve your wellbeing and the wellbeing of all those around you.

Once you read through the stress management techniques in this book, and apply them to your daily life, you will start to see some dramatic changes. You will feel more relaxed in stressful situations, and more confident in the face of things that once scared you. The heaviness in your chest and the anxieties that plague you will cease to bother you. You will be able to think clearly about the situation at hand, and stop overthinking.

Many people have thanked me for the positive impact that my training has had on their lives. These techniques have helped individuals lower their anxiety right away, and has also equipped them with the stress management tools they need to keep their anxiety levels low for the long-term. The continued success of this training program helped inspire me to write this book, and I am now able to present to you the same guide that I have given to so many patients. This book will provide you with a day-to-day program that is simple and easy for anyone to follow. It will also equip you with the knowledge you need to connect and understand the techniques listed. Anxiety and stress management doesn't have to be difficult or complex. In fact, many of the techniques I outline in this book are so simple that they sound ridiculous to many people when I first suggest them. But once you make these techniques a part of your daily life, you will begin to see how effective they truly are.

With my help and expertise, you will come away from this book fully equipped with the skills, techniques, and knowledge that you need to eliminate your stress and anxiety. You will also be able to manage your stress levels going forward, so that they never rise to a debilitating level again. My hope is that you will have all of the support you need to take back control over your own mental wellness, armed with all of the tools you need to change your life for the better.

Old habits die hard. It's a cliché, but it's true - and especially when it comes to our health and wellness. Another true cliché: human brains are like sponges, in that they constantly soak up information and stimuli from the world around us. Over time, bits of information sink deep into our subconscious, where they form our attitudes, beliefs, and habits. The longer these attitudes and habits go unchallenged, the more fixed they become in our minds, and the more difficult they are to change. This is great news if our attitudes and habits are beneficial, but it becomes bad news if we allow attitudes or habits that are harmful to enter our daily routine. However, just because something is difficult to change does not mean that it is impossible to change. The mental patterns that lead to stress and anxiety are psychological habits, ones that must be broken if you want to enjoy the valuable and significant moments of your life. Depending on how severe your anxiety is and how long you've struggled with it, overcoming these mental habits might be more difficult than you expect. But no matter what, the sooner you start applying these stress management techniques to your life, the easier it will be for you to overcome them.

And no matter how difficult it might be to apply these techniques, it's possible for everyone, at any level of stress, to successfully conquer their anxiety.

The guide that you are about to read has been proven over and over again to successfully help people overcome their stress - in any profession, and in any social situation. Each chapter of this book will provide you with practical, actionable steps that you can take to apply the research and psychological information to your daily life. These action steps will, over time, start to replace your old mental habits and behaviors. The closer you follow the techniques outlined for you in this book, the less you will think about them. Over time, they too will become habits, but ones that are instead setting you up for confidence and success - rather than stress, fear, or anxiety.

Chapter 1: Stressed? Join the Club and Get Started

If you feel stressed, the good news is that you're not alone. Stress is something that almost every individual experience at one point or another. Chronic fatigue, a short temper, or constant worrying are all common symptoms of extreme stress - experienced by thousands of people from all walks of life. Stress can come from a number of different sources, including your job (or lack thereof), your finances, your personal life, or your schedule. Feeling like you don't have enough time to finish all that you need or want to do is also a common source of anxiety.

In today's world, *stress* and *anxiety* are hardly uncommon words. From bestselling books, to podcasts, to news articles - it seems like everyone on earth is struggling with some kind of stress or an anxiety-related problem. In fairness, our modern world exposes us to far more media than our ancestors ever consumed. But the contemporary concern about stress may not simply be the inevitable result of saturation in more information. In fact, there is quite a bit of research to suggest that stress and anxiety are on the rise for many other reasons. For example, in 1910, it was reasoned that the average housewife spent about 52 hours a week on housework (Elkin, 2013). But in 1970, despite increases in machine efficiency, that figure was exactly the same (Elkin, 2013). Modern technology and infrastructure may have saved time for certain activities, but it also increased the demand for others. The time saved was instead filled with new and different responsibilities, and the workload has been kept essentially the same (Elkin, 2013).

Now, in 2020, we have even less free time than we did in the 1970s, let alone the 1910s. Whether you're a housewife, a doctor, or an artist, modern technology has simply increased professional and personal expectations of how much work you can reasonably achieve in a single day. Not only do we have far more to do now, but we have much less time in which to get it done.

In 2010, a study by the American Psychological Association (APA) found that 44% of Americans surveyed had experienced a significant increase in stress in the past five years (Elkin, 2013). That same APA study also found that 22% of adults believed themselves to be in fair to poor health, and that the stress levels reported by that group were significantly higher than the rest of the population. Just a few years later, a Harris Interactive study found similar results, where 46% of participants reported that they had experienced a significant increase in stress in the past five years (Elkin, 2013). The Harris study also found that a shocking 80% of people surveyed had reported medium or high levels of stress in the workplace, and 60% of people reported experiencing similar stress levels at home.

So why is the world so stressful? Is it simply because we're busier than we were 50 years ago? In part, yes, but those recent studies aren't just seeing an increase in stress over generations. People are reporting significant increases in stress after just five year periods. Part of the answer can also be found in Alan Toffler's text, *Future Shock* (1970), wherein Toffler found that people experience higher levels of stress when they are exposed to a lot of change in a short amount of time. Fifty years later, we can see the truth in his findings. What have the past few decades been but a constant stream of change? Think of how different the world was - even just 10 years ago. It can be exhilarating to live in a state of continuous change, but it can also make you feel out of control of your own life. More than ever, people live with these extreme levels of uncertainty. This chronic uncertainty can make you feel threatened, at worst, and overwhelmed, at best.

One of the biggest challenges in recent years was the 2008 economic crash. In 2010, just two years into the economic recession, an American Psychological Association study found that 76% of participants reported "money" as a significant source of stress in their lives (Elkin, 2013). At a close second, 65% of participants from the same study reported the economy as a significant stressor. Today, as world finances become more closely intertwined, the economies of all nations become increasingly unstable. The financial infrastructure laid down by past generations is unable to cope with new technology, new business practices, and new global trade relationships. The inevitable result of these large-scale changes is that, on an individual level, we have more insecurity about our money. Jobs may be created, changed, or disappear altogether. The regulations that govern credit, student loans, mortgage payments, and taxes will continue to evolve. As individual bills add up, the stress that we can feel around money continues to increase at a rapid pace.

It may seem that having a good, stable job would eliminate some of this financial stress, but a job can add additional stressors of its own. Job security, inconvenient hours, commutes, deadlines, difficult bosses, office politics, and disrespectful clients are just a few of the ways that jobs can add stress to your life. Even otherwise helpful and efficient technology can create workloads that are much heavier than they were 10 years ago - making even a "good" job stressful to perform every single day.

In 2012, a Harris Interactive study found that 41% of participants felt stressed during the workday (Elkin, 2013). In that same study, 58% of participants reported that they did not know how to successfully manage their stress. Today, those numbers have increased. It's now estimated that 62% of Americans experience a significant amount of job-related stress (Elkin, 2013). The economic cost of that stress, in terms of efficiency, medical bills, and loss of talent, is estimated to be around $300 billion nationwide (Elkin, 2013). A reported 25% of Americans have used their paid personal or sick leave just to get a break from the stress they feel at work, and the same number have reported feeling "often" or even "very often" burned out at their jobs (Elkin, 2013, p.12).

However, while money and work are two extremely common sources of stress, they are far from the only places stress can come from. In your journey toward better stress management, the first step is to determine the areas of your life where most of your stress comes from.

What are the Main Causes of Stress?

As mentioned, money and work are the two biggest causes of stress in the United States. In a 2015 survey conducted by the American Psychological Association, 72% of participants experienced high levels of *financial stress* during the past month, and 77% of participants cited finances as a source of extreme anxiety (Scott, 2020). Financial stress is such a pervasive and common source of stress that many people don't even realize how much time and energy they spend worrying about it. You know that finances are a significant stressor for you if you:

- worry or feel anxious about money
- argue with loved ones about money
- feel guilty about spending money
- are afraid to open letters or answer phone calls from banks and other financial institutions

Financial stress is considered so common because it can take years to overcome. If money is one of your major stressors, it is important to start now to manage your stress, as the effects are not just psychological. Long-term financial stress has been linked to a number of physical symptoms as well, including high blood pressure, headaches, stomach troubles, chest pain, insomnia, chronic fatigue, depression, anxiety disorders, skin problems, diabetes, and even arthritis.

After finances, *work trouble* is another significant stressor that plagues Americans today. According to a recent study conducted by the Center for Disease

Control and Protection, Americans today spend 8% more time at work than they did 20 years ago, and 13% more Americans work more than one job (Scott, 2020). Of participants in that same study, 40% reported experiencing extreme stress in the workplace, and 26% indicated that they often feel burned out at work.

However, a high volume of work is just one way that jobs can be stressful. Job insecurity can also be an extreme source of stress, as is dissatisfaction with your job or career. Conflicts with your boss or coworkers can also create a great deal of workplace anxiety. Whether you're treated unfairly or nervous about a major deadline, workplace anxiety doesn't always remain in the workplace. You often carry that stress home with you, where it can negatively impact your personal relationships. Workplace stress has also been linked to a number of physical and mental health symptoms, including chronic fatigue, headaches, muscle tension or pain, stomach problems, heart palpitations, anxiety, depression, and mood swings. Workplace stress can even negatively affect your cognitive abilities, which makes it more difficult to concentrate and make decisions.

You know that work is a significant stressor for you if you:

- use sick days even when you're not sick

- routinely underperform at work
- experience problems in your personal life
- have low creativity or motivation
- have low patience or high frustration levels
- find it difficult to become interested in new information or experiences
- socially isolate yourself

At one point or another, *personal relationships* will cause us to feel some level of stress. It's impossible to get along with everyone all the time. But a relationship can turn toxic when it is bad more often than it is good. Whether it's with a family member, a romantic partner, a friend, or a co-worker - a relationship that has gone sour can cause very high levels of stress. Relationship stress can sometimes be difficult to spot, as the individual stressors will be unique to the people involved. However, there are some relationship stressors that are more common than others. If you are feeling stressed by a close relationship, it may be because you or your partner:

- are too busy to evenly share responsibilities
- have other commitments that block your personal time together
- are not able to communicate clearly
- abuse alcohol or drugs
- have considered ending the relationship
- are overly controlling, manipulative, or abusive

Relationship stressors often manifest themselves physically as sleep problems, depression, anxiety, or chronic fatigue. You may start to avoid the other person, or become easily irritated by them. Either way, these stress-responses almost always make the situation worse, and thus increase your stress levels even more. Personal relationships don't always have to be face-to-face either. People that you communicate with primarily through social media can also be a significant source of stress. Bullying and miscommunication is much more likely to happen remotely than it is in person. Social media also causes you to unfavorably compare yourself to others, which creates stress and anxiety in its own right.

Another major source of stress is *parenting* - no matter how good your children are, or how much you love them. Inevitably, parents find themselves faced with incredibly busy schedules that ask them to juggle children, jobs, and household duties. Perhaps the worst symptom of parental stress is that it can cause you to become harsh, negative, or even authoritarian with your children. All of these stress-responses can decrease the quality of your relationship with your child, and therefore increase your levels of stress.

Busy schedules are far from the only source of parental stress. Financial instability, long working hours, single parenting, tension with your partner or co-parent, or raising a child with physical or cognitive disabilities can all be sources of stress. Parents of children with disabilities are at the highest risk for parental stress, and often report much higher levels of stress than parents of children without a diagnosis or a disability (Scott, 2020).

As well, being *over-scheduled* is an increasingly common stressor in our contemporary lives. Too much to do can cause you to become disorganized and unfocused, which leads to small mistakes like lateness or the loss of important items. A number of factors contribute to being over-scheduled, such as working more than one job, which can stretch out the workday and increase your daily responsibilities. Others may find themselves with too much on their plate because they connect saying "no" with a sense of guilt. Disappointing others carries a significant social energy. You know you're overscheduled when you put off basic tasks like eating or exercising because you "don't have time."

Determining Your Stressors

To help you identify the major stressors in your life, take out a piece of paper or open a blank document on your computer. Divide the paper into two sections:

Internal Problems and *External Problems*. All of life's stressors can be loosely divided into these two categories.

On one side, begin with the heading "*Internal Problems*". This will include all stressors that are related to you as an individual. Physical, psychological, and emotional stressors are all internal stressors because they affect you personally. Beneath this heading, leave space to list the following stressors: *Health*, *Relationships*, *Personal Beliefs*, *Emotions*, *Life Changes*, and *Money*. Put the items that cause you the most stress at the top of your list, and the items that cause you the least stress at the bottom.

Put a star next to *Health* if you are worried about aging, the diagnosis of a new disease, or symptoms and complications from a preexisting illness. These are all common stressors. Health also doesn't have to be about you. If a loved one struggles with an illness or condition, consider where you place Health on your stressor list.

Put a star next to *Relationships* if you have had an argument with your partner, parent, or child in the past month. Conflicts in other relationships can be stressful as well, so consider any outside of those three. But conflict or tension with the people that you live with can be even worse than conflict with people outside the home.

Put a star next to *Personal Beliefs* if you have had an argument about personal, religious, or political beliefs in the past month. Discussing these topics can be positive opportunities for growth - even if those discussions get lively or heated - but if you would categorize the discussion as a fight or an argument, then it was also a situation that caused you stress. If you have these kinds of arguments a lot, then *Personal Beliefs* may be something that causes you a significant amount of social stress.

Put a star next to *Emotions* if you find it difficult to relate to other people, or if you have experienced a traumatic event in the past. Emotional problems can have a number of different sources and can cause distress by themselves. But when our emotional troubles start to negatively affect our relationships, we start to feel a great deal of stress that can be related to feelings of guilt, inadequacy, or depression.

Put a star next to *Life Changes* if you have experienced the death of a loved one, started a new job, or relocated to a new home recently. All major life events bring their own levels of stress, from a child in college to retirement. Only you can determine the significance of these events, and where to place *Life Changes* on your list.

Finally, put a star next to *Money* if you carry significant credit card debt, are worried how to pay your rent, or are worried how to provide for your family. Money troubles can take many different forms, but these three stressors are the most common and, unfortunately, difficult to solve. Familiar solutions like a change in workplace or financial support from loved ones is helpful, but difficult to sustain in the long term.

Now take a look at your list. No matter what, you should focus on the top three items you placed on your list, as these three items were deemed significant by you - and this is important. However, all starred items need attention, and if you starred more than four items on your list, then you should consider *internal* stressors as your primary source of stress. If so, this is the area where you need to focus the most energy when it comes to stress management.

Now, move to the second half of the page, and begin with the heading *"External Stressors"*. These are stressors that come from social or professional sources, places that we often have very little control over. Beneath this heading, leave space for three items: *Occupation, Discrimination, Environment.* Write them in order of significance, with the first item being the highest stressor and the last item being the lowest stressor.

Place a star next to *Occupation* if you typically work more than 40 hours a week, or if you've experienced conflict at work in the past month. The American Psychological Association estimates that 60% of Americans experience extreme levels of work-related stress, so if this stressor is number one or two on your list, you're far from alone (Legg, 2016). Job-related stress can come from many sources, but long hours and workplace conflict have been the most closely linked to physical health consequences, and are most likely to negatively impact your personal and professional lives.

Put a star next to *Discrimination* if you have experienced physical, emotional, or social distress because of your race, ethnicity, gender identity, sexual orientation, or any other identity you have. Discrimination can cause extreme amounts of external stress, as it can prevent you from receiving professional opportunities, strain your social relationships with people outside of your identity group, and even put you in physical danger. Discrimination, while felt locally, primarily occurs on a large-scale social level, and has far reaching consequences, including limiting opportunities for the disenfranchised. While unfortunate, the roots of discrimination often lie far beyond what an individual person can change by themselves, and thus exist as an external stressor, rather than an internal stressor. However, this raises an interesting case. In America, being white, being born an American citizen, or living as male can all endow significant social privileges, including some that are not always noticeable. If you fit these categories, then yes, jokes about white people may make you uncomfortable; as may jokes about "Americans". But your reaction to these particular social situations should be considered internal stressors, not external stressors. It might annoy you when someone talks about how terrible men are, but that's not a situation that puts you in danger or disenfranchises you on a broad, social scale - and thus there is no external stress placed upon your experience - it is an inner reaction.

Finally, put a star next to *Environment* if you feel unsafe in the neighborhood where you live or work. Feeling unsafe can cause huge amounts of stress, making it impossible for you to relax when you are in that environment. Safety concerns can come from many different places, including crime, discrimination, or even environmental pollutants.

Now, take a look at your list. The first item you placed on your list should be your largest focus going forward, as that area of your life causes you significant levels of stress. If you starred more than one item on your list, then you should consider External Stressors as a major cause of stress. Looking at both lists, if you starred more than four *Internal Stressors* and more than one *External Stressor*, then you experience high stress levels throughout multiple areas of your life. If that's the case, then it is especially important to focus on your major stressors (top three for *Internal*, top one for *External*). If you learn to successfully manage stress in these areas, you will experience a significant amount of relief, and possibly even make it easier for you to cope with stress in other areas of your life.

Chapter 2: Do You Understand Stress?

You've now successfully determined the main sources of stress in your life. But what exactly *is* stress?

Psychologically speaking, stress has historically been defined in two ways: *stimulus-based* or *response-based*. The stimulus-based definition of stress suggests that stress comes from pressure. The greater the pressure, the more stress you feel. We can all tolerate low levels of stress. Our brains would be pretty poorly designed if we couldn't! But there is a certain point when the pressure becomes too much, and your mind and body start to suffer under the strain. While stimulus-based stress builds primarily from external stressors, it can then also relate to internal stressors - a cumulative nature of stress. In other words, the build-up of many tiny stresses can be just as harmful as one big, traumatic event (Butler, 1993).

The response-based definition of stress, on the other hand, suggests that stress specifically comes from negative stimuli. This approach focuses less on what causes the stress, and instead focuses on the severity of your body's reaction to stressors. This definition explains why something that might be exciting or even trivial to one person may be an extreme source of anxiety for another person. The ways in which the body responds to stress were first divided into three measurable stages by Hans Selye in the 1950s. According to his research, the first sign of stress in the body is what he called an "alarm reaction" (Selye, 1956). Today, we commonly call this the "fight-or-flight" response. Essentially, this is what happens when your brain registers a potential threat. Whether that threat takes the form of an oncoming train, a looming rent payment, or a gory scene in a horror film, your brain and body will respond in the same way. Once a threat is detected, your brain starts to produce different chemicals, and asks all of the systems of the body to be on high-alert so that you have the strength, energy, and alertness you need to deal with the situation. The stress response is, in theory, an amazing survival tool. It transforms us into superbeings, and heightens all of our senses in order to combat danger. But if you are in a constant state of stress, then the stress response never goes away. Your body never has the chance to go back to its normal "rest-and-digest" state, where you can relax.

If you sustain a fight-or-flight reaction long enough, your body goes into the second stage of stress, what Selye calls "resistance" (1956). In this stage, your brain is in conflict with itself. Your conscious mind knows that you are not in immediate danger, but your subconscious mind is not convinced. Unfortunately, it's the subconscious mind that triggers and subdues the stress response. You may be able to convince yourself that everything is fine, but it takes a lot more than willpower to convince your body. This is the stage where you start to treat your stress in order to relieve it. But there are healthy and unhealthy ways to cope with stress. If we are not fully aware of what happens inside our body, we can easily fall into negative coping methods like anger, manipulation, or avoidance. If this resistance stage continues for too long, your body will enter the third stage, what Selye calls "collapse" or "exhaustion" (1956). It is at this point that you start to see physical or mental health problems appear, which are directly related to your stress.

We know now that both definitions of stimulus-based and response-based stress are useful and important. It is very important to know where your stress is coming from, but it is also important to understand why you respond to your stressors the way that you do. Your personality, life circumstances, past traumas, and sometimes your genetics all combine to determine what pressures cause you to feel stress and the methods you naturally reach for to cope with your stressors.

Stress is dependent on two factors: the *demands* being placed on you by the situation, and the *resources* that you have to meet those demands (Butler, 1993). If the situation asks you to do more than you are capable of, then you start to feel stress. The catch, however, is that *demands* and *resources* are not objective words. Unfortunately, stress is not based in reality, stress is based in how you personally perceive the situation. Your thoughts, attitudes, beliefs, and fantasies all combine to create a unique understanding of yourself and your situation. If you believe that you are not able to meet a challenge, or not capable enough to successfully navigate a situation, then you will begin to feel stress. This occurs even if your belief is unfounded or simply untrue. Stress, then, can be seen as a kind of relationship. A relationship between you and the world around you. Stress arises when something in your life, whether it's another person, a bill, or a workload, drains you of all your resources and therefore puts you in danger (Lazarus & Folkman, 1984). The danger of unemployment, divorce, or the inability to provide a good home for your children are all very real situations that can trigger your body's stress responses. It could even be the threat of physical danger, like exhaustion.

Because stress is about how you perceive a situation, and not just the situation itself, there are as many different kinds of stressors as there are humans in the world. What makes you shrivel up inside with dread might seem mundane or boring to someone else. Something that makes you feel excited, or projects that you enjoy working on, might set another's teeth on edge. There's no such thing, then, as a stressor that's "not a big deal." If the situation causes you to feel stress, then it's a big deal to you. It doesn't make you weak or incapable, it's just a part of who you are. The solution is not to "stop" feeling stressed about something, rather, the solution is to figure out what it is about that situation that is causing you to feel stressed. Anxiety and stress mean that something about the situation in front of you feels threatening. For whatever reason, you feel like you don't have the time, energy, intelligence, or finances to handle the task in front of you. That is the feeling that we call "stress," and that is what we need to know within ourselves.

The Study of Stress

Stress is something we talk about so much that often we don't take a step back to think about what it really is. If you had to describe stress, what would you say? What words would you use? How is stress different from anxiety or worry? Sure, these distinctions might seem more important to a psychologist than to us. But the ability to understand exactly what the feeling of stress is, and how it might differ from other feelings, is very important to help us manage our stress appropriately.

While a common word now, the word "stress" first entered the English language in the 1300s. When it was first used, it was simply a shortened alternative to the word "distress," and was used primarily to describe physical hardships like pain, torture, or starvation (Stress Definitions from Stress Researchers, 2013).

Of course, the 1300s were a long time ago, but the meaning of the word stress did not truly change until more recently, in the early 1930s and the beginning of modern psychology. In an attempt to better understand how different states of mind can affect our mental and physical wellbeing, psychologists began using the word "stress" to relate to mental and emotional hardship, not just physical pain. Hans Selye was one of the first to define stress in psychological terms, calling it a "non-specific response of the body" to change, or to the perceived need for change (1954, p.1). In other words, the first psychological definition of stress tells us that stress can indeed take many different forms. It also tells us that stress is a response to change, or when you feel like a change needs to be made, such as a deadline, an unpaid bill, or relationship pressure.

Selye continued to research stress, and eventually developed his three stages of the stress response - fight-or-flight, resistance, and collapse (1956). But later, in 1979, he changed his definition slightly, calling stress instead a "perception" (Stress Definitions from Stress Researchers, 2013). In other words, stress became understood as subjective. Not necessarily related to reality, nor a purely physical sensation, but stress instead begins in our mind first. Selye would continue his research and later clarify further, stating that stress does not necessarily occur with all life changes, but it occurs when we feel we have to make a change and we don't know how to successfully achieve it (Albrecht, 1979). For example, if a major deadline looms, you know that you need to work faster. But you don't know how to work faster without burning yourself out. The result? Stress. Consider also the stress that comes when you plan a wedding - there are so many things to be done that you don't even know where to start!

It was in 1982 that the psychologists Holroyd and Lazarus suggested that stress could also be measured in terms of your "resources" (1982). For example, if a situation demands more time, money, or energy than you have available, you may develop more stress (Stress Definitions from Stress Researchers, 2013). If, on the other hand, you have enough resources to successfully navigate a situation, then you may feel something else, possibly a feeling of confidence or excitement. You may also not even feel anything at all, and catalogue it simply as a mundane task.

But in 1985, another shift occurred in the scientific world. J.E. Skinner suggested that rather than stress as an internal development, it was instead a reaction to negative, external forces (Kunos & Ciriello, 1992). This created our "stimulus-based" definition; to counter the earlier "response-based" definition (Stress Definitions from Stress Researchers, 2013).

We know now that both of these definitions have grains of truth to them, but the final piece of the stress puzzle wasn't found until 1988, when R.S. Eliot expanded upon the Holroyd and Lazarus definition (Stress Definitions from Stress Researchers, 2013). It was Eliot who first suggested that the stress response was not triggered by how many resources you have, but about how many resources you *think* you have. So stress may be triggered by external events, but it develops internally as a response to those events. Two people with the same resources, one who believes they have enough and another not enough, will feel different levels of stress. In short, it's not the situation itself that causes stress, but the way that you respond to it.

But the story of stress doesn't end there. In 1990, Steinberg and Ritzman determined that stress actually took two basic forms: "overload" and "underload" (Stress Definitions from Stress Researchers, 2013). If you feel overloaded with information, whether too many choices, too much to do, or too much input from other people, then you will begin to feel stress. This idea connects well to Selye's original theories from the 1970s. If you feel overloaded, then your stress is not from feeling incapable of succeeding, but rather, from feeling stuck or confused about the appropriate next step.

On the other hand, you can be underloaded if you feel you do not have the resources to cope with the task in front of you, even something as common and familiar as washing the dishes or answering a text. When you look at your own stressors, consider whether you feel overloaded or underloaded. Do you have too much on your plate? Do you feel completely overwhelmed by the situation(s) in front of you? Or are you afraid that you don't have what it takes to successfully handle the situation? Do you feel that you aren't capable enough?

Just a few years later, in 1992, James Humphrey united overload and underload stress under one common title. Humphrey stated that stress was caused by anything that makes it difficult to maintain "equilibrium" (Stress Definitions From Stress

Researchers, 2013)). So whatever disrupts your internal feelings of competence and peace, by this definition, can be considered a cause of stress. These are what we now refer to as "stressors." Whether you feel underloaded or overloaded, you have encountered a situation where it is increasingly impossible for you to feel at peace (Stress Definitions from Stress Researchers, 2013). Your stress response has been activated, and you can't seem to make it go away.

What are the Symptoms of Stress?

You now have a better understanding of what stress actually is, at least from a psychological standpoint. But what are the symptoms of stress? How does stress affect our mental and physical wellness?

Contemporary science understands that what Selye called the "collapse" phase of stress is a very real, physical phenomenon. When your brain feels threatened, for any reason, it will first have your nervous system release a number of different hormones, including adrenaline and cortisol. These hormones are called stress hormones; their job is to change your body chemistry so that you can respond to the threat in front of you. When stress hormones are released, your heart pounds faster, your muscles tighten, your blood pressure rises, your breath quickens, and you become more alert. In the short term, these changes greatly increase your strength and stamina. But in the long-term, they can have some serious side-effects.

Stress can negatively affect any system of the body. It's not only a psychological phenomenon. Worse, stress can aggravate pre-existing health conditions, making them much worse or causing flare-ups from conditions that were once under control. Sometimes stress can even cause us to develop conditions that we are genetically susceptible to. Conditions that can be triggered or worsened by chronic stress include (Segal et al., 2020):

- depression and anxiety disorders
- pain
- sleep disorders
- autoimmune disorders
- digestive disorders
- skin conditions (eczema)
- heart disease
- weight problems
- reproductive disorders
- thinking and memory problems

Stress can trigger a number of different conditions throughout the mind and body, even if you are not necessarily predisposed. Not everyone experiences all of these symptoms, and they also have much to do with your situation, lifestyle, mindset, and coping mechanisms.

The most common *cognitive symptoms* of stress are memory problems, inability to concentrate, and poor judgement (Segal et al., 2020). Chronic stress makes it nearly impossible for your brain to focus on what's in front of you because you constantly worry about the stressor. And if what's in front of you *is* the stressor, then you can only worry about what might happen if things go wrong. To properly process new information, your brain needs to maintain a certain level of attention. If you're not focused, it becomes difficult for your brain to store new memories. As such, people who are extremely stressed often forget information or misplace important items, like car keys.

Many people who deal with chronic stress often find it difficult to think positively. Anxious or racing thoughts can sometimes develop, as can a state of constant worry. These symptoms are especially common in people who also have depression or anxiety disorders. All of these symptoms can create further problems in your life, not just in the immediate stressful situation. The more problems you have, the more stressed you become, trapping you in a vicious cycle.

The most common *emotional symptoms* of stress are depression, general unhappiness, anxiety, agitation, moodiness, irritability, and anger (Segal et al., 2020). People who would not otherwise consider themselves depressive or unhappy can find their mood dangerously darkened by chronic stress. Sometimes that stress can develop to the point that it becomes a major depressive episode. Another condition that can be brought on by stress is anxiety, even in someone who otherwise would not consider themself an anxious personality. In fact, stress is so often the trigger for people developing anxiety disorders that the two words are increasingly being used interchangeably. In today's world, with stress on the rise, it is hardly surprising that the number of people diagnosed with anxiety disorders also climbs year by year.

Even if you are not diagnosed with a mental health disorder, stress can still cause you extreme emotional distress. Stress can cause you to feel overwhelmed, lonely, and isolated. By themselves, these feelings are terrible to live with. Over time, these feelings can also develop into mental health problems, even after your stress has gone away. Emotions are powerful forces in the brain. If you spend a long time feeling overwhelmed, that emotion becomes deeply rooted in your view of the world - even if the original cause of that feeling is long gone.

The most common *physical symptoms* of stress are aches and pains, diarrhea and constipation, and nausea or dizziness (Segal et al., 2020). It is extremely common for people dealing with chronic stress to visit the doctor's office and complain of inexplicable aches and pains before they ever visit a psychologist. Unfortunately, it is still unclear whether the phantom pains caused by stress have a direct physical cause, or if they are low-level hallucinations. As well, diarrhea or constipation are both as likely to occur because of the pressure chronic stress puts on the digestive tract. Eating well and exercising can help, but no matter how great your habits, stress can still stop your digestive tract from doing its job properly.

The stress response also elevates your heart rate, and for that reason, some people experience chest pains or heart palpitations when they feel stressed. Those chest pains are definitely not phantom pains. Victorian novels are filled with people who die from fright, lovesickness, or shock, and strangely, those novels are not far from the truth. The strain that chronic stress puts on the heart and circulatory system can absolutely lead to heart disease and in extreme cases, can include cardiac arrest. Loss of sex drive can also occur with chronic stress, as can sexual dysfunction. Those whose immune systems are suppressed may find themselves constantly sick, contracting every cold, flu, and virus that comes their way.

The most common *behavioral symptoms* of stress are eating disorders, sleep disorders, and social withdrawal (Segal et al., 2020). A common response is stress eating, where someone eats, or constantly snacks, but not because they're hungry. Rather, they eat because it triggers the release of serotonin in the brain. Serotonin is a chemical that makes us feel good, bringing a stress eater some temporary emotional relief from the stress they feel. However, stress eating can lead to all kinds of health problems, including rapid weight gain, digestive disorders, and heart disease. Stress eaters rarely reach for salads - instead, they're far more likely to reach for "comfort foods" like ice cream, chocolate, mac n' cheese, or a big juicy hamburger - which can release greater serotonin levels.

On the other hand, stress can also cause someone to lose their appetite altogether. They either forget to eat because they're busy with the problem in front of them, or they intentionally stop eating because they just don't feel like it, or have the energy for it. Either of these habits can lead to a number of different health problems, and can make it far more difficult for the body and brain to cope with other stress-related symptoms.

No matter what symptoms you may experience, they are probably extremely unpleasant. And if you have not noticed any of these symptoms yet, it may be only a matter of time before you do. These symptoms are the primary reason why stress is so detrimental to our health and wellbeing, and halting the progress of these symptoms is the main reason it is so important to manage your stress as early as possible.

Chapter 3: Managing Stress - The Basics

Though stress can wreak havoc on your life, a stress management strategy can seem overwhelming in its own right. Almost always, when I first recommend stress management to people, their first response is that they don't have time, they're too busy, it's too much work, or, most commonly of all, that they've already tried stress management and it didn't work.

But none of these things are true. At least, not if you don't want them to be. If you feel like you don't have the time or you're too busy to manage your stress, don't worry. It's okay to go slow, and go at a pace that works best for you. There are no deadlines in stress management. If you only have 10 minutes a day to spare, that's fine. If you only have 10 minutes a week to spare, that's fine too. The only important thing is to stay committed and put yourself on a regular schedule. Don't tell yourself you'll do it "whenever you have time." If you do that, you'll never get around to it, and give up before you've really even started.

Stress management is a skill, and like all skills, it takes time and practice to learn. You can't master it overnight, no matter how hard you try. So you might as well go slow. Overwhelming yourself will actually increase your stress - the opposite of what stress management is supposed to do. For ideal results, 15 minutes a day is the recommended time to devote to a daily stress management technique (Avoiding Roadblocks to Stress Reduction, 2016). This might sound like a long time, but that 15 minutes can happen during a coffee break, a lunch hour, the moment that you get home from work, or during your morning commute.

If you are resistant to taking on a new project or feel like stress management is simply too much work, just remember that there is no one right way to manage your stress. Everyone's stressors are unique, and everyone's idea of relaxation is different. A beach in the Caribbean might sound like heaven to you, but it might sound like hell to someone else. Don't be afraid to drop or modify a stress management technique if it doesn't work for you. But remember, it may take awhile before many of these techniques start to show results. If you begin to dread your designated 15 minutes of daily meditation, try instead to experiment with different kinds of meditation, or even move on to a different technique entirely.

That being said, try to keep your mind open and give new things a try. Some of these stress reduction techniques might feel a little strange or uncomfortable at first. Some may be familiar to you, while others might be completely new. With increasing amounts of stress in the world, different stress management techniques may have gained mainstream attention. This is both a good and a bad thing. For example, you may have heard of breathing exercises before, or even tried a few of them yourself. But the context in which you were introduced to this concept can sometimes affect the way that you think about it. Try to have an open mind, and give these techniques an honest try before you rule them out. You might be surprised at what starts to work for you once you find a way to work it comfortably into your daily routine.

Most methods and techniques require practice before you get them completely right. Approach stress management the same way you would approach learning to ride a bike or drive a car. You won't do it perfectly the first time. Or the second. Or even the third. Though stress management can seem like an intellectual pursuit, it's not enough to only read about it. Anyone can understand how to drive a car from a simple explanation. But to get behind the wheel is a different kind of learning. When you try out a stress management technique, you get behind the wheel, so to speak. So be patient, be open, and eventually you will get into a style and rhythm that is comfortable for you.

It is very important to practice stress management techniques in a quiet place. Don't wait until you're in a stressful situation to apply these tactics. Think about it like learning an instrument. You need to practice every single day, so that when the day of the concert arrives, you already know what to do. Stress management keeps your stress levels low all the time, so that when you are faced with a stressful situation, you're able to keep calm and confident. However, a quiet place can be difficult to find if you lead a hectic and busy life, so you might have to settle for places that are less glamorous. If you have your own office, that's a great place to practice undisturbed. If you have your own bedroom, that's another good option. Wherever you choose, try to find a space that's relatively private, where you won't be disturbed by others.

Don't feel the need to embark on this journey alone! If someone else in your life is also dealing with stress and anxiety, ask if they want to practice with you. Many self-care routines, like weight loss or going to the gym, are far more effective when you have someone else to do it with. Stress management is the same. You won't feel as alone or self-conscious if you have someone else to practice with, and you're far more likely to stay committed if you have a friend to cheer you on.

Above all, don't expect overnight results. The stress you're experiencing took years and years to build, and so it may take just as long to completely overcome. That's not meant to scare or discourage you, however.

Stress management doesn't have to be an invasive or difficult process, but no matter what, it will be a slow one. Don't get impatient with yourself, and don't be too quick to give up on something that isn't yielding the results you want. Go slow, go easy, and don't be too hard on yourself.

How to Measure Your Stress

How can you measure a feeling? Fortunately for doctors and psychologists, stress isn't just something you *feel*. It also affects your behaviors and your physical wellness. For doctors, stress levels can be easily tracked by looking at physical markers, including blood, urine, and even saliva tests that measure the levels of stress hormones present in your body (Figueroa-Fankhanel, 2014). But stress can also be measured from a psychological perspective. Some methods, like observation and interviews, are conducted by professionals. But there are a number of easy strategies you can employ to measure your stress levels on your own. The following 3-Step Process is a very simple one that will help you check in on your own stress levels. It will help you be more aware of how stress affects you, and help you keep track of your progress as you begin employing techniques for stress management.

1. Do a Gut Check

It may seem obvious, but the first step in measuring your stress level is to simply take a step back and ask yourself, "How do I feel?" A gut check is simply giving yourself a second to check in with your body and mind and determine how you're feeling. Remember that stress presents in everyone's body in slightly different ways. If you find yourself feeling stress, take a moment to observe the situation. How would you rate your stress, on a scale from one to ten (one being very low, ten being extremely high)? Think about your physical symptoms. What's happening in your body? Do you feel pain or tension anywhere? Are you experiencing digestive troubles? Are you having trouble performing sexually? Understanding where and how stress is stored in your body will help you to understand just how stressed you are in any given situation. Sometimes we become so used to dealing with stress that we don't even realize how severe our stress is until our body presents with physical symptoms.

Next, observe your mood. Are you feeling depressed? Anxious? Angry? Just as different people's bodies express stress differently, your mind expresses stress in unique ways too. Learning how you emotionally respond to stress is just as important as learning what your physical symptoms are. Some people become extremely depressed when they're under a lot of stress. Other people feel extremely nervous or anxious. The ways that you emotionally respond to stress will give you clues as to what steps are best for you when it comes to managing your stress successfully.

2. Use a Stress Gauge

The most commonly used psychological tool to measure stress levels is called the Perceived Stress Scale, or PSS. If you're someone who likes specificity and you want a more concrete way to measure your stress, there are a number of PSS tests and tools available for free online from reliable websites. This test will give you a number between 0-40 to determine how severe your stress levels are. The test asks you to think about your life over the course of the past month, and so it's most useful when conducted on a monthly basis.

3. Make Yourself a Stress Journal

This can be a physical notebook, a document in your computer, or a dedicated desk drawer. Whatever form it takes, your stress journal is going to be your most important tool as you move forward with your stress management journey. Keeping a record of your stress levels will help you to determine if your stress management techniques are working, and will give you valuable information about yourself that you will need to make the necessary adjustments. Keeping notes in your stress journal does not have to be a difficult task. All you need is 5 minutes a day to update your journal and check in with your emotional and physical wellbeing.

Every day, the first thing you should do when you open your stress journal is rate your stress on a scale from 1-10. This is your gut check, your own personal score. How would you rate your feelings of stress today? If you like, on the first day of every month, take an online PSS test. Pay attention to how your score changes over time. If it's going down, what techniques have you been using that are successful? If it's going up, maybe it's time to change the way you're using your chosen techniques or even try some new techniques altogether.

Once you've recorded your daily score, make a list of any negative physical symptoms you've experienced that day, including pain, fatigue, or other health problems. Finally, write down one word that you would use to describe your mood. Naming your feelings is extremely important for your mental health, but if it's not something you're used to doing, it can sometimes be difficult to find the right words. If you're struggling to describe your emotions accurately, you can find a mood chart online that you can use to help you label your feelings every day.

Recording your stress levels, mood, and physical symptoms every day will give you a lot of information to work with. At the end of your first month, you will be able to look back at your journal and see patterns emerging. You might notice that you usually record having a headache when your stress levels are high. You might notice that you feel irritable all the time, but you only experience anxiety when your stress levels are high. You might find that you were feeling extremely depressed until you started meditating, but once you started that technique, you haven't been feeling so down. Taking just five minutes a day to check in with your feelings can be a stress-reducing technique on its own. Having awareness of how you're feeling and what's going on in your body is perhaps the most important thing you can do when it comes to managing your stress. The unique physical and emotional ways that your body responds to stress is called your "stress signature." Like your fingerprints or your handwriting, your stress signature is unique to you. The more you understand how your body responds to stress, the better you will be at successfully managing it.

Managing Your Stress - The Three-Step Method

Now that you've checked in, determined your major life stressors and created your stress journal, you're ready to begin taking some real steps to manage your stress levels. The simplest stress management approach is called the Three-Step Method (Manage Your Stress: A Three-Pronged Approach, 2016). Stress management is really about finding a way to manage three different things: your stressors, your thoughts, and your stress responses. Different techniques target different categories, but the best way to manage your stress is to find a balance between all three. Stress management is about finding out how your stressors, your thoughts, and your responses all work together to produce the stress that you feel every day. Only focusing on one or the other will only help you to solve one part of the problem.

The Three-Step Method for Stress Management:

1. **Manage Your Stressors**

Often, stress management techniques focus on eliminating or reducing the events, people, or situations that cause you stress in the first place. While this is not always possible, it is still very important to understand where your stress is coming from in the first place. Stressors can be huge life events like divorce or illness, or small inconveniences like a broken shoelace or a crowded subway. The way that you respond to a stressor won't always correspond perfectly to the severity of the stressor itself. If you experience chronic stress, sometimes a small event can trigger a big response.

Earlier in this book, you completed an exercise to determine where the major sources of stress in your life were coming from. Now it's time to go back to those categories. Look at your major stressors and break them down into specific incidents that you can change or modify. For example, if "work" was a major stressor for you, take a moment now to break "work" down into specific examples. What exactly is it about work that stresses you out? Is it your crowded commute? Are you constantly late? Are you generally dissatisfied with your job, company, or department as a career path?

Now that you've made your list, think about how you can turn these "stressors" into "modified stressors." For example, if you have a crowded commute, is it possible to leave the house earlier or later? If you are constantly late for work, determine what makes you late. Do you need to wake up earlier? Do you need to establish better boundaries with the people you live with in the morning? Do you need to arrange for a more reliable mode of transportation?

We are careful to call these "modified stressors" instead of "solutions" because you don't know if they'll work until you try them. Leaving the house 15 minutes earlier than normal might turn your nightmare commute into a dream. But it also might be difficult for you to wake up that early. You might find that your roommate's car blocks you in, or that 15 minutes is not enough time to catch an earlier train. Your solution might solve part of the problem, but it might not completely eliminate your stress. That's okay! Creating a list of modified stressors gives you a better understanding of what you do and don't have control over in your life. It helps you to think creatively about resolving the situations that cause you stress, rather than becoming further and further trapped in feelings of frustration or anxiety. Breaking your stressors down into small, specific situations can also help to make those situations seem more manageable. "Work" is a huge category, with many potential problems and stressors. But "missing deadlines" is a specific problem that can be solved with specific action steps.

2. Manage Your Thoughts

Remember that stress isn't caused by external events. It's caused by how we *perceive* those events. You might find that there are certain stressors that you have very little control over. You can't always avoid being stuck in traffic or an encounter with unpleasant people. But the way that you think about your situation can go a long way to manage your stress. Change the way that you see a stressful situation and sometimes eliminate your stress altogether!

The next time you find yourself in a stressful situation, try to observe your thoughts in the situation. If your thoughts are negative ("Oh my god, what am I going to do? I hate this. I can't believe this is happening..."), then you might need to tackle the way that you think about the stressful situations in your life, especially if they are situations that you can predict. If you hate your long or crowded commute, try to find a way to make it more enjoyable. Make yourself a commute playlist or listen to an audiobook while you sit in traffic. If you have lots of medical appointments, use the time you spend in the waiting room to practice a foreign language or watch an interesting video on YouTube. Whatever the situation may be, try to see what you can gain or learn from it, rather than obsess over how much you hate or dread it. Put all the mental energy that you put into your worry into your enjoyment. At the very least, you can imagine how good you'll feel when the situation is over!

3. Managing Your Responses

This is where stress management techniques come in. You may not be able to change your stressor, and while positive thinking is always powerful, there are some situations whose silver-linings just aren't bright enough to make a real difference in your stress levels. Techniques like meditation or deep-breathing are techniques that manage the way that your body responds to stress. Meditation won't make your situation disappear, and it may not change your perspective on it. But it will help to reduce the depression or anxiety that you feel in your mind, relieve the physical tension that you feel in your body, and restore your cognitive abilities so that you can continue to work toward solutions. Managing your stress responses often takes the form of lifestyle changes, like exercise or eating healthy. The techniques that you choose can also specifically target your individual responses. For example, if you tend to get headaches when you feel stressed, you might try stretches or breathing exercises that release tension in the neck and shoulders that cause tension headaches. If you experience digestive issues, try to modify your diet to give your gut the extra nutritional support that it needs to keep you happy and healthy in your time of stress.

Chapter 4: Get Rid of Stress and Anxiety

At this point, you've identified your major stressors, you've made your stress journal to record your physical symptoms and emotional responses to those stressors, and now you are ready to apply real techniques. Any and all stress or anxiety-reduction techniques have one ultimate goal - relaxation. This is especially true for techniques that target our thoughts and responses to stressors that we have little control over.

Relaxation is essentially the difference between a successful stress-management technique and an unhealthy coping strategy. Successful stress-management relieves tension in the body and mind, and helps you to face your situation with confidence and a clear head. Coping strategies, on the other hand, cause us to experience even more fear and tension. Avoidance is a big coping strategy that many people employ because it solves the problem in the short-term. But procrastination, ignoring problems, and cancelling commitments, while they remove the stressful situation in the moment, have a way of creating even more stress later on. Other coping strategies like lashing out at others in anger, pulling an "all-nighter" to get projects done on time, or numbing yourself with drugs and alcohol may also seem like confronting the problem, but they too make your situation much worse.

Relaxation is the core of stress management because it both helps you to relieve the negative symptoms of your stress and helps you to approach difficult situations with confidence. Relaxation relieves the tension in your body, while it also heals and prevents the negative physical effects of chronic stress. It also lifts your mood, clears your mind, and shields you from the negative emotional and cognitive effects of stress. Relaxation is how you relieve your negative feelings without an attempt to escape or suppress them. Once you've released the tension from your mind and body, you can then approach your problems with a clear head, instead of merely succumbing to fear responses.

There is nobody who doesn't want to feel relaxed. But the number one obstacle to a successful incorporation of relaxation techniques is time management. Often, people feel stressed because their lives are busy. If you have too much on your plate, then relaxation techniques can seem like just one more item to add to your list, one that you may not be able to prioritize over other items that you feel are more important.

However, relaxation techniques do not have to be an invasive part of your day. If you feel like you have too much to do, then a second look at your schedule could be a simple technique to manage your stressors all by itself. But the most important thing to remember is that relaxation is... well, important. Really important. Relaxation techniques incorporated into your daily routine will improve your ability to perform every single task on your To-Do List. It will also improve your mood, the quality of your relationships, and your general feelings of happiness and wellbeing. Through the relief of physical tension, relaxation techniques are also beneficial, and perhaps even necessary, for your physical health. If you can find the time to brush your teeth or take a shower every day, then you can definitely find the time to focus on relaxation.

To successfully use these techniques, the first thing to do is set aside a specific time every day for relaxation. It doesn't matter if it's in the morning or at night. It doesn't matter if you'll be at home, at work, or even in your car. The idea is to choose one specific time for relaxation so that nothing else can take precedence over it. If 10:45-11am is your set relaxation time, then nothing else should be scheduled during that time - no meetings, no phone calls, no hanging with friends. Keep this in mind when you set your relaxation time. It's best to choose a time when you can be by yourself in a quiet space and control any unexpected interruptions. For this reason, most people find that the first 10-15 minutes after they wake up or right before they go to bed are the best times for relaxation, but only you can know which time is best for you.

I have suggested 15 minute blocks, but if that seems like too much, you can set aside as little as 5 minutes a day for relaxation. Many techniques are simple, and require no preparation or props. Some people prefer to set themselves several 5 minute relaxation blocks throughout the day. Others would rather give themselves 15-20 minutes every day. Again, there's no right or wrong answer, as long as you're consistent and committed. No matter how long it is, when your relaxation time comes, put everything aside and focus on your chosen technique. That being said, your relaxation period should be practiced daily. Unfortunately, your body doesn't store relaxation. So a daily relaxation practice of 5 minutes will be much more effective than if you employ a relaxation technique once a week for a full hour (Davis et al., 2008).

If you struggle to find an appropriate time to relax, ask yourself two questions: When do I need to relax the most? And when can I break away from external demands to take some time for myself? If you find it's a struggle to get ready or motivated in the morning, then you might want to practice relaxation right after you wake up, or even in the car on your morning commute. Many people find that relaxation in the morning helps them to face the day with confidence, and even helps motivate them to get moving in the morning when they would normally be sluggish.

However, other people have found that relaxation in the middle of the day provides a welcome break from the stress of their busy schedule. Take a quiet moment during a lunch break or simply close your office door for 10 minutes so that you can remain undisturbed. This will help you relieve whatever stress has built up during the day. It can also help you to handle stressful situations faster, and return to your day feeling calm and refreshed. A popular time for many people is just before they leave for work, or right after they come home, especially if work is a major source of stress for you. Relaxation just before you go to bed is another popular time, especially for people who experience sleep problems as a physical symptom of stress.

Relaxation: The Basics

Relaxation is the opposite of stress. Relaxation techniques allow your body to come out of its flight-or-flight response, soothing and even eliminating the symptoms of stress. Relaxation techniques have been proven to slow your heart rate and lower your blood pressure. They slow your breathing rate, improve your digestion, and can even help you to maintain healthy blood sugar levels. No matter what your stress symptoms are, relaxation can help to relieve it. Relaxation brings your body from fight-or-flight into a state called rest-and-digest. Your body stops the production of stress hormones and increases blood flow to the muscles, which in turn relieves pain or tension in those areas.

But relaxation doesn't just relieve the physical symptoms of stress. It improves your concentration, mood, and sleep quality. Daily relaxation practices have been linked to higher energy levels, lower levels of anger and frustration, and greater confidence and self-esteem. And the best part is that all relaxation techniques work equally well. You don't need to choose a specific relaxation technique to help your digestion, nor one to lift your mood, nor one to lower your heart rate. Relaxation techniques are holistic, which means that they heal the entire body all at once. Whatever symptoms you experience, you only need to choose one technique to heal *all* the symptoms of stress present in your body.

There are a few different kinds of relaxation techniques to choose from. If you're like most people, you'll find that some techniques work better for you than others. That's okay! No technique is "better" or "worse" than any other. It simply depends on your unique body, attitude, and stress signature.

Autogenic Relaxation

Autogenic is a word with Greek roots, and means "something that comes from within" (Mayo Clinic Staff, 2020, "Relaxation..."). Autogenic relaxation techniques use visual imagery and awareness of the physical body to reduce your stress. Often, these techniques ask you to repeat a certain word or phrase in your mind that helps you to relax, especially in your muscles. A common example is to imagine yourself in a peaceful setting, and then focus on controlled, relaxed breathing in order to slow your heart rate. Some autogenic techniques ask you to focus on specific parts of the body and relax your muscles one by one.

Progressive Muscle Relaxation

This technique asks you to tense and then relax individual muscles, one-by-one, until the whole body is relaxed (Mayo Clinic Staff, 2020, "Relaxation..."). This technique is especially good for those who experience muscle tension or pain as a physical symptom of stress, but it's worth it for anyone to try, regardless of their stress signature. After they try this technique, many people find that they *do* in fact experience tension in their muscles, but they were so used to that tension that they didn't even realize it! This technique helps you to become more aware of physical sensations in the body. It provides a greater understanding of how your body carries stress and which parts of your body are particularly sensitive to stress. Often these techniques will ask you to start with your toes and work your way up, or start at the top of your head and work your way down. Typically, you tense your muscles for five seconds, and then release them for thirty.

Visualization

This technique asks you to imagine a peaceful place or situation to help you feel safe and relaxed, no matter where you are in real life (Mayo Clinic Staff, 2020, "Relaxation..."). Visualization techniques incorporate all of your senses; imagine smells, sights, sounds, and feelings that are pleasant and comforting to you. For example, if the ocean is a place where you feel peaceful and relaxed, don't just imagine what the sea looks like. Try to hear the sound of the waves, smell the salt water, and feel the warm sun on your skin. Visualization techniques are most easily done with your eyes closed in a quiet spot. It's often recommended that you wear loose or comfortable clothing when you visualize. Many visualization techniques will also ask you to focus on your breathing.

More Advanced Relaxation Techniques

The previous three techniques are the most basic and universally accessible, but they are far from the only relaxation techniques available to you. Again, no technique is "better" or "worse" than any other. Just because a technique is more advanced doesn't mean it will work better. Don't overlook any technique until you've given it a try. You may find that a simple technique is the most effective for a complex problem. That being said, if those three techniques don't work for you (or if you simply want to expand your relaxation practice), there are many other techniques that have been successfully employed by people all over the world, from all walks of life.

Deep breathing is a technique that simply asks you to focus on your breathing. Breathing exercises often ask you to take deep, long breaths. Different breathing exercises can be more or less complex, but if you simply take five minutes a day to focus on breathing slowly and deeply, it can yield some amazing results.

Massage is often the first thing people think of when they think of relaxation, and there is a reason for it. Massages help to relieve stress-related tension in the body. Sometimes, chronic stress has caused our muscles to become so tense that they can't relax without external help. Massage therapists use a number of different techniques to help chronically tensed muscles to relax. In some cases, chronic muscle tension can even cause your bones to move out of place. Many massage therapists also help correct this, and ease your bones back into their natural place.

Meditation is another practice that has become more and more popular. Though it can take a variety of forms, meditation encourages you to focus your mind 100% on the present moment. Meditation can feel like a challenge, especially if you have a mind that likes to whirl and leap from thought to thought. But its benefits have been touted by people as varied as religious leaders, CEOs, psychologists, and artists around the world.

Tai Chi is a relaxation technique that has its roots in ancient Chinese medicine. Tai Chi involves slow, practiced movements, performed in a certain sequence, that help to release tension in both mind and body. Many people around the world feel comfortable with their own personal tai chi routines, but as a beginner, there are many videos online that you can follow to learn the movements.

Yoga is another relaxation technique that focuses on the flow of specific movements in order to relieve stress and tension. Yoga has its origins in India, but is currently practiced by millions of people all over the world. The movements of yoga are often more intense than those of tai chi, and sometimes involve deep stretches or complicated poses. However, there are many different kinds of yoga, and none of them need to be advanced. You can sign up for a class at a local yoga studio, or you can buy your own yoga mat and follow any of the thousands of instructional videos available for free online.

Biofeedback is a technique that has also become more and more popular as modern technology enables us to better understand how stress affects our brain waves. Biofeedback monitors your brain activity, and helps you to identify patterns of stress, relaxation, anxiety, and even mood states like depression or anger. This might sound complicated, but biofeedback monitors are increasingly available for purchase online, and at cheaper prices than you might think. The idea behind biofeedback is that, if you can learn to recognize stressed and relaxed brain states, then you can make much better adjustments to your lifestyle in order to promote relaxation and reduce stress.

Tips for Success

There are so many relaxation techniques out there, it can be hard to know where to begin or which ones might be the best for you. It is important to always be patient with yourself, and give something a fair try before you decide that it doesn't work for you. That being said, here are some tips that you can keep in mind to ensure success and make your chosen techniques more beneficial.

No matter which relaxation techniques you choose, it is advisable to do it in a cool and quiet space where you will not be disturbed (NHS Inform, 2020). While you certainly want to be comfortable, stress can increase your heart rate and actually cause your body temperature to rise slightly. Make sure that your relaxation space is cool to help lower your body temperature and make it easier for your body to calm itself down.

It is also advisable to lie down or sit on the floor with your legs crossed. Unless you've chosen a technique like yoga or tai chi that requires movement, it is rarely comfortable to relax while you stand or sit upright. Lying down is, of course, the most comfortable position of all, but many people find it beneficial to sit cross-legged because that's not something they normally do. Sitting on the floor can also become part of your relaxation routine, as it signals to the brain that it is time to calm down.

If you can, take off your shoes and try to wear comfortable clothing. Tightness and discomfort will make it that much more difficult for your body to relax. The more comfortable you are, the easier it will be for your body to release any pent-up tension. And the more pleasant you can make your relaxation time, the more likely you are to stick with it!

If you can, try to close your eyes (NHS Inform, 2020). This may intimidate you or even seem silly, but with your eyes closed you are free from any potential distractions in your environment. Even if your exercise is just breathing, close your eyes to help you focus purely on relaxation, and decrease the likelihood that your mind will start to wander. Increased focus can also speed up the relaxation process, and allow your body to settle into the technique more quickly.

Finally, regardless of what technique you chose, always try to focus on your breathing. Deep, slow breathing automatically calms your nervous system and floods your bloodstream with oxygen. It is very difficult to maintain stress and tension when your breathing is slow and deep. This is the reason that slow, deep breathing works as a relaxation technique all by itself, and is a critical element of any successful relaxation technique.

Depending on when and where you chose to practice relaxation, you may not be able to follow all of this advice to the letter. For example, it's impossible to close your eyes or sit on the floor if you've decided to relax during your morning commute. But if you don't see the results you want with your chosen technique, you may want to consider a change in your time, place, or method so that you can better incorporate some of these strategies. While these tips are helpful for any relaxation technique, there are some strategies you can try that are unique to specific strategies.

Success Tips for Deep Breathing

Anxiety can sometimes dramatically disrupt your ability to breathe, and cause you to feel faint, dizzy, or nauseous. If you choose a breath-based technique, or need assistance to regulate your breath during any chosen technique, there are a few things you can do to help yourself take even, regular breaths.

One easy way to check in with your breathing is to place one hand lightly on your chest, and the other on your stomach. You want your stomach to move slightly more than your chest when you breathe. When you place your hands on your body, it helps your mind to focus on that area, and makes it easier to pay close attention to your breathing patterns. With your hands on your body, you will also feel your heartbeat slow down, which lets you know that your focused breathing is working (Puddicombe, 2011).

If at all possible, try breathing in through your nose and out through your mouth. This kind of breathing helps to circulate air throughout your respiratory system, and helps to cool your brain and stimulate the major nerves in the throat. When your mind is focused on your breathing, it eliminates distractions and pulls your mind from its spiral into anxiety-inducing thought patterns.

Success Tips for Visualization

If you choose visualization as your preferred technique, or if you would like to incorporate visualization into another technique, you may find that it's sometimes difficult to focus on the suggested image. There is no right or wrong image to visualize, but no matter what, you want to create a mental picture of a space where you feel safe. This place can be real or imaginary, as long as it's a space where you feel rested and calm. This might sound obvious, but it's important to keep this in mind if you start to try visualizations or guided meditations. For example, if the ocean is an environment that stresses you out in real life, a guided meditation that asks you to imagine the coast or beyond is probably not a good choice for you.

Remember that visualization is most effective when it engages all of the senses (Puddicombe, 2011). If you struggle to maintain your visualization, try to move through your senses one at a time. Ask yourself, what does my comfortable place look like? What can I see? What can I hear, smell, or feel? The more sensory detail you can imagine, the more real your relaxation space will feel, and the more relaxed you'll feel.

Chapter 5: Relaxation Tips

As more and more people experience high levels of stress and anxiety, more and more people are also invested in sharing techniques for relaxation. Once you choose the technique you want to try, it's extremely easy to find the guidance you need online to do it entirely by yourself. However, the wealth of information out there can be overwhelming for some people, and sometimes it's hard to know which sources are reliable. For this reason, I've compiled some easy exercises and a variety of techniques to help get you started. I would recommend that you try all of these techniques at least once to better understand what works best for you. Once you become more comfortable with a specific technique, you will feel more confident to branch out and perform your own research.

Breathing Techniques

Exercise #1 - Simple Belly Breathing

Sit in a comfortable position on the floor with your back straight and your legs crossed. Place one hand lightly on your chest and the other over your stomach.

Breathe in deeply through your nose. Feel your hands move as your body expands with air. The hand on your stomach should move slightly more than the hand on your chest.

Exhale through your mouth, releasing as much air as you possibly can. Contract your stomach muscles slightly to push out as much air from your lungs as possible. As you exhale, the hand on your stomach should move inward toward your body, while the hand on your chest should move very little.

Continue to breathe in deeply through your nose and out through your mouth for the duration of your relaxation time. Pay attention to the movements of your hands as they rise and fall with each breath. Mentally count to ten each time you exhale.

If you find it difficult or uncomfortable to sit up, you can do this same exercise while comfortably on your back. If you would rather lie down, you can choose to put a small healing stone or crystal on your stomach instead of resting your hand there.

As you breathe deeply from your belly, you stimulate the vagus nerve, the longest nerve in the body. Stimulation of the vagus nerve helps your body to lower your heart rate, and in the long term, helps to lower your blood pressure.

Exercise #2 - Deep Breathing with Affirmations

Find a quiet place to sit comfortably and close your eyes.

Breathe in deeply through your nose, and exhale through your mouth. Repeat this three times.

When you take your fourth breath in, imagine that the air you're breathing is filled with peace and calm. You can even imagine breathing in a relaxing color, bits of stardust, or any other image that you associate with positivity and tranquility.

When you next exhale, imagine that you're breathing out all of the stress and tension stored up in your body. You can even imagine that your exhale is a noxious color or thick like mud. Whatever you imagine negativity to look like, imagine it leaving your body.

On your next, fifth inhale, think of a word or phrase that fills you with peace, calm, and confidence. It can be something as simple as "I breathe in peace and calm," or as specific as "I'm allowed to change my mind about people," or even something empowering like "I can do this!"

When you exhale, repeat your affirmation to yourself. Continue to repeat your affirmation with each inhale and exhale for the duration of your relaxation time.

Body Scans

Exercise #1 - Body Scan Meditation

Lying down is the best position to perform a body scan, but if that's not comfortable or possible for you, then this meditation can also be easily completed while you sit up in a comfortable position.

Take a deep breath through your nose, and exhale through your mouth. If you find your shoulders rising and falling dramatically with each breath, try to focus on breathing from your belly rather than your chest. Take three deep, belly breaths.

Continue to breathe slowly and deeply, but now shift your attention to your feet. Observe any sensations you feel in your feet. No matter what you feel, whether it's pain, tension, comfort, heat or cold, try to simply observe and accept it. Take note of any sudden emotions that come up in response to the feelings in your feet.

If you notice any feelings that are uncomfortable, focus on them now. Continue to breathe slowly and deeply. With each exhale, imagine all the pain, tension, or discomfort that you feel leaving your feet and evaporating into the air.

When you're ready, slowly move up your body, and repeat this practice of awareness until you have gone all the way up to the top of your head. Spend two or three breaths becoming aware of each part of your body, but spend extra time anywhere that you experience pain, tension, or discomfort. After you've finished the meditation at the top of your head, record in your stress journal anywhere that you noticed pain or tension in your body. The next time you perform this relaxation technique, check if you experience discomfort in the same areas.

Exercise #2 - Quick Top Down Body Scan

Lay or sit comfortably in a quiet place.

Close your eyes. Breathe in deeply through your nose, and exhale through your mouth. Repeat this three times.

Now bring your awareness to the top of your head. Notice any sensations that you experience there. Remain aware for three full breaths, and simply notice how you feel. If you experience any pain, tension, or discomfort, stay there for three more breaths. With each exhale, imagine the pain or tension leaving your body to evaporate into the air.

Now move your awareness down your body, and spend at least three full breaths on each area of the body. Spend three extra breaths anywhere in your body where you experience discomfort, and visualize the tension leaving your body. Once you have finished the meditation with your feet, record any areas where you felt pain or tension in your stress journal. If you finished the meditation before the end of your relaxation time, return to each of the parts of your body that experienced pain or tension. Lay your hands gently over the afflicted part of the body. Visualize warm, healing energy entering your body. Visualize the pain evaporating into the air like steam rising off the surface of warm water. Extend this visualization for the duration of your relaxation time.

Progressive Relaxation and Physical Meditation

Progressive Relaxation

Progressive relaxation is a technique that asks you to briefly tense and then relax individual muscles in the body. For these exercises, you will focus on different muscle groups, and move progressively from one to the next until you've relaxed all parts of the body. You can simply memorize the order of the muscle groups, or you can use an audio recording or cue cards to help prompt you to move from one group to the next.

Exercise #1 - Muscle Group Progressive Relaxation

To begin, lay down on the floor or on a comfortable bed. Take a deep breath in through your nose, and exhale through the mouth.

On your second inhale, tense the first muscle group, and keep the muscles tensed for 4-10 second, but not to the point of pain. When you exhale, suddenly and completely release the muscles. Don't try to gradually relax them. Unclench completely as soon as you breathe out, and enjoy the relief as tension leaves your body.

Simply breathe slowly and deeply for 10 to 20 seconds before you move on to the next muscle group. You will experience some feelings of relief every time you relax, but make a mental note of any muscle groups that feel especially good. These are places where you carried tension before you began the exercise.

Continue until you have tensed and released all muscles groups.

The Muscle Groups, and How to Tense Them (Freeman, 2009):

- Hands: Clench them
- Wrists and Forearms: Extend up from the body, and bend the hands back at the wrists.
- Biceps and Upper Arms: Clench the hands into fists, bend the arms at the elbows, and flex the biceps.
- Shoulders: Raise them up toward the ears.
- Forehead: Wrinkle into a deep frown.
- Eyes and Nose: Clench the eyes shut as tightly as you can (if you wear contact lenses, you should remove them while performing this exercise).
- Cheeks and Jaw: Smile as widely as you can.

- Mouth: Press your lips together as tightly as you can. Be aware of any tension that accumulates elsewhere in the face.
- Back of the Neck: Press the back of your head against the floor or pillow.
- Front of the Neck: Touch your chin to your chest.
- Chest: Inhale deeply through the nose, and hold your breath for 4-10 seconds.
- Back: Arch your back up away from the floor or bed.
- Stomach: Suck in the muscles as tightly as you can. Be aware of any tension that appears in the chest or lower back.
- Hips: Press the buttocks together as tightly as you can.
- Thighs: Clench the muscles as tightly as you can.
- Lower Legs: Point the toes back toward your face. Then point your toes downward, and arch your feet. Be aware of any tension that appears in the thighs or hips.

Exercise #2 - Top Down Progressive Relaxation

Find a quiet and comfortable place to lay down. Inhale deeply through the nose, and exhale through the mouth. Repeat this three times.

Now bring your awareness to your forehead and the top of your head. Notice any tension in the muscles there as you breathe in. On the exhale, intentionally and suddenly release that tension. If you don't feel some relief, repeat this procedure one more time.

Now move progressively down the body, and bring your awareness to the muscles in each part of your body. Anywhere that you experience tension, intentionally and suddenly release it on your exhale. Take an extra breath in areas that experience extreme amounts of tension.

Once you've finished the exercise at your feet, record in your stress journal any areas that you felt were particularly tense. The next time you repeat this technique, compare your notes. Were the same areas carrying tension?

Physical Meditation

Tai Chi - The Basics

Tai Chi is a form of physical meditation that comes from an ancient Chinese spiritual practice called Qi (or Chi) Gong. The "chi" in both of these words comes from a Mandarin Chinese word that loosely translates into English as "spirit" or "energy." In traditional Chinese medicine, your chi is your body's life force, the vital energy that flows throughout your body, healing and restoring your organs and muscles. According to Qi Gong, if chi becomes sluggish or clogged in its journey through the body, then you become sick, both physically and mentally. All Qi Gong meditations are focused on moving chi more fluidly throughout the body.

This might sound like a bunch of hocus pocus, but modern medicine is discovering greater links that connect the concept of chi with a sound scientific basis. We now understand that all parts of the body are interconnected, and that pain or tension in one part of the body can lead to negative physical symptoms throughout multiple organ systems. We also know that our psychology is intimately tied to our physical bodies. Mood states like depression, anxiety, and stress can express themselves as physical symptoms of illness.

Tai Chi is essentially a sequence of practiced, fluid motions that are designed to move chi throughout the body. A focus on the slow, measured poses of tai chi takes your mind off of your stress and brings awareness to your physical body. Daily tai chi practice has been increasingly linked to a number of different physical and mental health benefits, a major one of which is stress reduction. As tai chi becomes more popular in the west, it has become easier and easier to find tai chi classes in local yoga studios, meditation centers, and gyms. There are also a number of tai chi instructional videos online that you can follow for free in the comfort of your own home.

Yoga - The Basics

Perhaps the form of physical meditation most commonly practiced around the world is yoga. Though many people see yoga as a kind of exercise, this practice originated in India as a form of meditation, and knowledgeable yoga instructors will bring a spiritual element into their classes, no matter how much of a sweat you work up.

Yoga can appear quite intimidating to beginners, but it does not have to be difficult or strenuous. A simple yoga flow will take you through a series of stretches, and the instructor will often guide your thoughts toward positive images or phrases to think about as you move through the flow. An extremely popular practice around the world, most cities and towns have a local yoga studio where you can take a variety of classes with licensed instructors, and maybe even meet some like-minded people. There are also thousands of free videos that you can follow online in the comfort of your own home. All you need is a yoga mat, some comfortable clothes, and a full water bottle.

Visualization Techniques

Exercise #1 - Simple Visualization for Building a Safe Space

Find a quiet space where you won't be disturbed and take any posture in which you feel comfortable and relaxed.

Breathe deeply in through your nose, and exhale through your mouth. Repeat this three times.

On your fourth inhale, close your eyes. Imagine yourself in a beautiful location, where everything is perfect, peaceful, and utterly relaxed. There is no right or wrong place to imagine, as long as it's somewhere that brings you total comfort and relaxation. You can imagine yourself on a beach, a mountain, in the middle of a forest, or even inside a building.

Imagine yourself calm and relaxed in that space. You can imagine yourself smiling, laughing, sleeping, or doing anything else that you would do if you were completely at peace.

Focus on the sensory details of your space. What do you see? What do you hear, smell, or feel? If you're a food lover imagining yourself eating a delicious meal, what are you eating? What does it taste like? All of the sensory details in your space should be aesthetically and physically pleasing. Spend time with each of the different senses, and fully imagine the details of your safe space.

Remain within this space for the duration of your relaxation time.

Exercise #2 - Inner Beach Visualization

One of my favorite places to be is on the beach, and it appears that I'm not alone. Many people have found that visualizing themselves next to the ocean is a scene that fills them with peace and tranquility.

To visualize your inner beach, find a quiet place where you won't be disturbed. Take any posture that feels comfortable and relaxed.

Close your eyes. Inhale deeply through your nose, and exhale through your mouth. Repeat this three times.

On your fourth inhale, imagine yourself on a beautiful beach. Look out at the sand. What color is it? Take a handful and run it through your hands. Is the sand rocky or smooth? Are there seashells or seaweed along the coast, or is your beach miles of pure, well-kept sand?

Now look out at the water. What color is it? Is it clear turquoise? Dark blue? Gentle green? Steely grey? Look up at the sky and make the same observation. Is the sky purely blue and cloudless? Is there a bright sun or is it a starry night sky? Is there a gorgeous sunrise or sunset on the horizon? Is it overcast? Perhaps you love the romance of rain or weather over the ocean?

Now imagine the sound as the waves hit the sand. Time your inhales and exhales to match the rhythm of your inner ocean waves. Remain comfortably on your inner beach for the duration of your relaxation time.

Chapter 6: Calming Your Mind

Anxiety is a psychological condition that can arise from many different sources. For many people, anxiety and its spectrum of disorders develop as a response to stressful or traumatic experiences. But anxiety also has a genetic component. Some people are genetically predisposed to be more likely to develop anxiety disorders than others. Anxiety can also be passed from a mother to a fetus during pregnancy, regardless of genetics. If a mother experiences extreme stress or anxiety during pregnancy, the stress hormones in her body can affect the way that her baby's brain develops (Haas, 2017).

Whether it comes from your environment or your genetics, anxiety is something that deeply affects the way that your brain works. Anxiety can actually restructure your brain, to the point where anxiety disorders are visible on brain scans. However, studies done at Harvard Medical School have also proven that certain relaxation techniques can similarly restructure your brain, much like the "rewiring" effect of anxiety. Using a number of different research methods, the Harvard studies have demonstrated that relaxation techniques, when practiced daily, change the way that your brain processes information, and can transform anxious neural pathways into calm ones (Haas, 2017).

When anxiety becomes "wired" into your brain, it means certain neural pathways develop in your brain in response to stressful situations. Over time, your automatic response to certain stressors is to experience fear, anger, and distress. Your brain immediately goes into fight-or-flight mode when faced with certain stress triggers, even if the situation at hand is not actually dangerous or threatening. So when it comes to your brain, your strongest defense against anxiety is to develop what Harvard researchers call a "relaxation response." This can be achieved when you develop a daily relaxation routine. Just as anxiety causes your brain to enter fight-or-flight when faced with certain stressors, a daily relaxation practice trains your brain to return to rest-and-digest. So, for example, if you take ten minutes every morning to practice deep breathing while you listen to calm music, your brain will learn to relax when you start the practice. Slowly but surely, your brain will begin to anticipate relaxation time. As your designated relaxation time approaches, your heart rate will automatically start to slow, your blood pressure will decrease, and your body will start to come out of its high-stress state.

Regardless of the relaxation technique that you choose for your designated practice time, it is always beneficial to practice deep breathing any time you begin to feel anxious. Anxiety disrupts your natural breathing patterns, and causes you to breathe more quickly and shallowly. In the short term, this is intended to help your body conserve its energy to fight off danger. But in the long term, this can cause your brain to become under-oxygenated, and inhibit your ability to think clearly or regulate your emotions. So if you recognize that you feel anxious, take a second or two to breathe in deeply through your nose and out through your mouth. Even just a few rounds of slow, deep breathing can train your brain to stop the release of stress hormones in the body.

However, sometimes it can be hard to recognize when you're anxious. Fears and worries have a way of gnawing at us, occupying our subconscious minds even when we try our best to think about anything else. If you're a chronic worrier, you may want to consider scheduling a "worry time". Just as you schedule yourself a relaxation time, schedule yourself five to ten minutes everyday to think about your worries. This may sound like strange advice, but if you try to bury or ignore your fears, it rarely makes them go away. Instead of letting those fears take over your life, give yourself ten minutes a day to obsess, plan, imagine the worst case scenario, cry, rant, or do whatever else you need to do. For this moment, give into your worries and fully experience your fears. Then, when your ten minutes are up, dry your eyes, clear your throat, and get on with your day. If you find that you start to worry outside of your designated time, stop yourself. Tell yourself to think about it during tomorrow's "worry time".

An alternative strategy is to schedule time to write down your worries and fears in your stress journal every day. When you write, you force your brain to slow down, which stops you from a spiral into pits of anxiety and nervousness. It can also be cathartic to take the time and write down your fears. As your thoughts leave your mind, and fall onto paper, it serves a similar function as venting to a trusted friend. The difference, however, is that the act of writing is private. Sometimes it can be difficult to relax and fully release your thoughts when someone else is present, no matter how strong your relationship with that person may be. If you take the time to slow things down, you are provided with a safe, and completely private way to open up and unleash the thoughts that truly eat away at you. When done just before bed, this technique has been proven to be especially helpful for people who suffer from anxiety and stress-related insomnia (Haas, 2017).

How to Cultivate a Calm State of Mind

A daily relaxation technique greatly contributes to improvement in your emotional and psychological stress symptoms. However, it's also useful to employ simple tactics throughout the day to keep yourself in a calm state of mind. You want your brain to be your friend. You don't want your ability to think to be regulated by your anxiety.

Breathing is something that we humans take for granted, but it can't be stated enough how powerful and valuable breathing is for your body and mind. Slow, deep breathing activates your parasympathetic nervous system. This is the part of your nervous system that regulates unconscious processes in your body. The parasynthetic nervous system controls automatic functions like your heartbeat, digestion, and hormone production. When this part of the nervous system is engaged, your body naturally moves into rest-and-digest mode. When relaxed, your body will typically enter this state. However, rest-and-digest mode is far more important than it sounds. Only in this state can your body heal itself from physical and emotional harm. If your body is in stress mode instead (fight-or-flight) - it cannot fight off diseases, repair wear-and-tear on your body, or filter out toxins. In stress mode, all of these processes are suspended. These processes can only be accomplished when your body is relaxed and your brain feels calm.

Just a few deep breaths when you start to feel anxious or worried can stop your brain from entering fight-or-flight mode. The psychological and emotional power of deep breathing has been most dramatically demonstrated in its effectiveness for military veterans. The trauma and post-traumatic stress that combat veterans experience is so severe that 50% of veterans do not see significant improvement with therapy or medications (Seppala, 2019). However, many studies have found that after just one week of daily deep breathing exercises, veterans suffering from PTSD, including those who were unable to improve their condition through other methods, showed noticeable improvement in their mental wellbeing (Seppala, 2019).

Another recent study found that your breathing patterns change depending on the emotions that you experience. The study recorded the specific breathing patterns common in people who experience anger, fear, happiness, relaxation, and other emotions. Researchers then taught these breathing patterns to a new group of people, who were not given the context of the breathing exercises. When researchers asked the new subject group how they felt after they completed a few minutes of their designated exercise, the participants' emotional responses corresponded almost exactly to their breathing patterns (Seppala, 2019). Many participants who had been taught the "angry" breathing pattern reported feelings of anger or frustration after breathing that way for a few minutes, even though none of them knew that the breathing pattern they had been taught was related to feelings of anger (Seppala, 2019). In essence, the test subjects were able to evoke certain emotions through a change in their breathing patterns. So, taken another way, a focus on slow, deep breathing can also have a direct effect on your mood. Breathing in a "relaxed" pattern tricks your brain into actual feelings of relaxation!

Breathing in through the nose and out through the mouth is encouraged in most deep breathing exercises because it stimulates the vagus nerve, part of the parasympathetic nervous system. As mentioned in the belly breathing exercise from Chapter 5, the vagus nerve is one of the longest nerves in your body - and a significant portion of this nerve is connected to the muscles in your throat. So, the act of breathing in through your nose and out through your mouth can activate the vagus nerve, while circulating air throughout your respiratory system. This, in turn, activates parasympathetic nerves throughout your entire body, which reduces your heart rate and eases your body down into rest-and-digest mode.

Remember, however, that stress and anxiety are not just physical responses. These emotions are psychological responses, too, so their origin is not just external. A number of studies have connected self-criticism and low self-esteem to severe anxiety and depression. The more you beat yourself up, the more anxious you become as a person. A harsh inner voice and a low sense of self-worth can severely inhibit your ability to solve problems or tackle challenges. Anxiety often arises from a feeling of powerlessness or inability to adequately solve the problem at hand. More often than not, the belief that you aren't able to succeed comes from your self-esteem, not from an objective evaluation of your talents and abilities. If you don't believe you can succeed, then you probably won't, because instead of focusing all your energies into solving the problem at hand, your brain becomes overwhelmed with anxiety, self-hatred, and depression.

Therefore, another important strategy to cultivate a calm state of mind is to practice self-compassion. Don't be so critical of yourself. Nobody is perfect. Everyone makes mistakes. The problem is that our competitive modern society often leads us to believe that failure means we've done something wrong. Instead of learning from our mistakes in order to better ourselves, we see our mistakes as examples of why we're not good enough, smart enough, attractive enough, etc. We allow our mistakes to hold us back, when we should instead use them to propel ourselves forward toward success.

Affirmations are positive words and phrases that you repeat to yourself whenever you feel anxious or insecure. These affirmations are an extremely effective strategy to improve your sense of self-worth. Whenever you feel anxious, depressed, stressed, or frustrated, repeat your chosen affirmation to yourself in your mind, or even out loud. It can be anything, even something more general like "I can do this," something that will apply to almost any situation. You can also make specific affirmations for specific fears or stressors. For example, if you tend to be extremely self-critical about your physical appearance, your affirmation might sound something like "I will find one beautiful thing about myself every time I look in the mirror." The more you repeat your affirmation to yourself, the more you will start to believe it. Slowly but surely, the tone of your inner voice will start to change. Rather than self-criticizing, you will start to self-encourage, which will equip you with a mindset of confidence and resilience and greatly reduce the power of your stressors.

Chapter 7: Organization and Time are Key

No matter how busy or stressful your life may be, your system of organization and your schedule should be designed to best support you so that you can finish what needs to be done. If you constantly lose things, forget things, or show up late to commitments, then it's time to take a second look at how you structure your life. Chronic stress can shorten your attention span and make it difficult to focus, so your forgetfulness may be a symptom of stress. But no matter how well your system works for you, if you're constantly unable to function in times of stress, then that system needs to be adjusted. The extra stress of scrambling at the last minute is not something that you need in your life.

Organizing the Home

No matter where in your life your stressors originate, a cluttered living space can add to stress and anxiety levels. Clutter in the home can make it more difficult for your brain to focus, and therefore, more difficult for your body to relax - even if you consider the home to be a safe and comfortable space (Scott, 2019). Clutter in the home can also drain money from your budget and time from your schedule. This can take the form of lost or broken items, time spent hunting for important items like car keys and paperwork, or difficulty moving around easily in your own space. This, in turn, can create more stress in your finances or make it more difficult to successfully manage your time.

Organizing a home can feel like a formidable task, but there's no need to tackle your entire living space all at once. Instead, make a note in your stress journal every time you lose something, forget something, or show up late. Write down what it was that you lost or were late for, and the reason that it happened. For example, if you were late to work because you spent twenty minutes on the hunt for your keys, make a note of that. Where did you ultimately find your keys? Would it be valuable for you to have a designated key space? What room did you look for your keys in? If that room was less cluttered, would you have been able to find your keys more quickly? You may not have to re-organize your entire house - you may just need to reorganize the kitchen or hang a magnetic key-hook on your refrigerator. Focus on the small goals.

Time Management

Time management is essentially the art of organizing your time. If you constantly rush around, or show up late to places because you have way too much on your plate, then your schedule is in need of a second look. Many busy people feel that there is nothing they can do about how busy their schedule is. They have a lot to do, and they think they just have to roll up their sleeves and try their best to get everything done.

But the reality is that you have more control over your schedule than you realize. The first and most important rule of good time management is to not overschedule yourself. When you make a To-Do list, don't simply write down what you have to do, but also record how long it will take you to do it. Whether your task takes you five minutes or two hours, also schedule yourself an extra ten minutes for unexpected changes, interruptions, or challenges. If you have more items on your To-Do list than you have time to complete, determine if there are any items that you can eliminate, push to a later date, or delegate to someone else. You're not superhuman. If you try to push yourself to get more done than you have time for, you will only create more problems. Not only will it increase your stress levels, but it will decrease the quality of your work and your ability to focus.

If you don't already have a physical To-Do list, then it's time to make one! Whether it takes the form of a calendar, a notepad, or a spread-sheet - it doesn't matter. If you only keep all your tasks and commitments in your head, you will increase the likelihood to forget something important and cause yourself more stress. A written, physical To-Do list will help you prioritize tasks, and ensure that you get the most important items done first. Items that are less important you can either eliminate from your schedule entirely, roll over to an easier day, or delegate to someone else. It can be very difficult to determine which of your tasks are important if you spend all of your energy trying to remember everything that you have to do.

Finally, don't just schedule tasks like work, doctor's appointments, or meetings. Schedule yourself some downtime as well. No matter how much energy you have now, if you never give your mind and body a chance to rest, you will eventually start to burn out. It might seem like a waste to schedule yourself time to rest and relax everyday, but you will find that you are a lot more productive if you give yourself an adequate amount of time to rest, engage in self-care, or have personal time with a loved one.

Organization as Stress Management

Sometimes stressors are related to organization in ways that we don't even realize. For example, if you listed work as one of your major stressors because of your crowded commute, try to take a step back. When you sit in traffic and start to feel stressed, what causes that stress response? Almost always, people with stressful commutes are stressed because they do not want to be late for work. This common, work-related stressor is something that can be solved with organization. You can't change the amount of traffic on your commute, but can you leave the house a little earlier in the morning? If possible, talk to your boss about an adjustment to your work hours. Is it possible for you to start a bit later in the morning, and leave a bit later in the afternoon? Is it possible to do the opposite? Often, we have no control over certain stressors in our lives, but organization is something that we definitely have control over. Whenever you feel stressed, take a mental step back. Is there a way that you can adjust your schedule or your physical environment in order to eliminate this particular stressor?

The relationship between organization and stress isn't just about smoothing over logistics. Your brain constantly scans your physical environment and looks for signs of potential danger or other situations that might require some kind of energy investment on your part. If your surroundings are chaotic, your brain can sometimes decide that you are in danger, which then triggers the stress response (Voltolina, 2017). The same is true if your mindset is fragmented. If you constantly break your concentration to frantically find a paper that you misplaced, or remember the address of the doctor's office, then your brain registers this fractured mental energy as a sign that you're in a situation that requires more energy than you currently have (Voltolina, 2017). And if you perceive that you don't have enough resources to successfully navigate the situation in front of you, that triggers the stress response, too.

Getting yourself organized is also a way to feel like you're more in control of a situation, and the feeling of control is a great way to help your body relax. Even if you don't create an active solution to your stressors, make time to get yourself organized and eliminate the stress that comes from a cluttered space or an overbooked schedule. The act of organizing itself can even be considered a relaxation technique, because it helps to make your physical and mental environment more peaceful. Strange though it may sound, cleaning your room can help to relieve work-related stress. Organizing your desk can put you in a calm mindset so that you're ready to face the relationship stressors you may experience at home.

That being said, it's sometimes the case that our organization strategies are the very things that cause us to feel stress! Because of the sense of control they give us, we can sometimes become over-dependent on our organization strategies. This might be you if you constantly work from nine different To-Do lists, or check your digital calendar every minute. Organizational strategies should help us to feel calm and relaxed. If your organization technique causes you to feel more stress, then it doesn't work for you.

It's great to have a well-organized schedule. But if your schedule is too tightly packed, then even the slightest change or surprise can throw off your entire day. That can obviously create a great deal of stress, but what's even worse is that your brain will start to constantly worry about the possibility of change or surprise. Your schedule, in that case, may help you to stay organized, but it also fuels high levels of anxiety and makes it extremely difficult for you to handle change or challenges in a healthy way.

The best schedule is one that allows for a little bit of flexibility. Always give yourself that extra ten minutes for every item on your To-Do list, so that when the unexpected does happen, you have that buffer time to handle it, and can possibly reschedule the other items on your list. That little bit of scheduled "padding" can go a long way toward the relief of chronic anxiety, and help you to feel more confident in the face of challenge. And if you end up with a bit of extra time at the end of the day, that's an added bonus!

You can also choose to break big projects into smaller pieces. This essentially breaks one big, high-stress deadline into many smaller, low-stress deadlines. Look at one big project as a series of small pieces to help you to feel more relaxed and in control as the final deadline draws closer. Each time you complete a small piece of the project, you will feel more and more relaxed in the knowledge that the overall project will be finished on time. It also makes us feel good to complete a task, or to check an item off your To-Do list. Each time you complete a piece of your project, you'll enjoy the boost of confidence that inevitably comes with achieving goals.

Organization - A Three-Step Approach

Organization for stress management can easily be broken down into three simple steps. Remember, organization should only make you feel better, not cause you more stress. If the idea of a reorganization of your home, your schedule, or your workspace fills you with anxiety, then don't try to tackle the entire project all at once. Instead, follow these three stages to get yourself organized in a way that both calms and empowers.

Three-Step Organization

1. Schedule Your Organization Time

Set aside a designated time every day to plan and organize. I find that most people prefer to schedule their organization time in the morning, but if you prefer to work at night or in the middle of the day, that's okay, too. Tasks to be done during this time may include: make your To-Do List, fill out your schedule, clean your desk, check your emails, or throw away clutter. Whatever you need to do to get yourself planned and organized, do it during your set organization time. Just ten minutes of organization time a day can go a long way toward less stress and more control of your life.

That being said, make sure that you put a time limit on your organization time. If you set yourself ten minutes, then once those ten minutes are up, it's time to move on to the next thing on your schedule. The goal is to create daily habits, not finish in a single day. But also be sure that you don't allow yourself to be trapped in your planner. The more time you obsess over your schedule, the more stress you will feel, and the less time you will actually have to get things done. Ten minutes a day is all you need to get yourself planned, oriented, and organized.

2. Prioritize your Efforts

A general To-Do list item, such as "clean the house," is unlikely to be an effective organization strategy because "the house" is a big place. Unless you have an extra five hours to spare in your day, it will be way more efficient for you to organize more specific areas of your life that are cluttered or chaotic. One strategy is to dedicate a specific area of your life for each day's organization time. For example, imagine that you set your organization time for 1:15-1:30pm every day. On your calendar, dedicate Monday's organization time to simply organizing your inbox, Tuesday to only conquering the junk drawer, Wednesday to finalizing your filing cabinet, and so on. Instead of an attempt to organize your entire life all at once, you only need to spend 15 minutes a day to straighten out a specific area that needs some extra attention.

Alternatively, you can schedule an entire weeks' worth of organization time for one big area. Still 15 minutes a day, but tasks from Monday to Sunday cover the same area. Again, the idea is to create daily habits, not simply finish a task. So you might spend all of this week's 15 minute blocks on the task to "organize your desk," while next week you will organize a different area of your house. However you choose to do it, the idea is to focus on one area at a time. This will make the task of organization seem a lot more manageable. And as you start to reap the mental benefits of living an organized life, you might even find yourself looking forward to your organization time!

3. Eliminate Paper

Without a doubt, paper is the worst culprit when it comes to clutter. Mail, bills, receipts, and other paper documents can create quite a pile-up. It can be difficult to sort through what's important and what's not, and it can be difficult to efficiently store the paper documents that you determine are worth saving. Paper storage units like filing cabinets or desk drawers can also take up a lot of space, and can become cluttered and disorganized in their own right if they aren't carefully maintained or frequently cleaned out.

No matter how you feel about digital technology, it can often be easier to organize documents digitally than it is physically. The more paper you eliminate from your space, the easier it will be to keep yourself organized and decluttered. Certain apps like Genius Scan are free to download to your smartphone, helpful in this case, and easy to use. These apps help you to digitally scan everything from receipts to documents and store them in the appropriate files on your phone. If you don't use your phone for document storage, you can always email the files to yourself and store them on your computer. Either way, it eliminates the need for paper, reduces the likelihood that you'll lose or misplace an important paper, and reduces the amount of space you need for document storage. Unlike physical filing folders, files on your computer can hold thousands of documents without an increase in size, and will automatically sort themselves alphabetically by the name of the file.

We all tend to grow stacks of "stuff" around our houses, those piles of paper or other junk that we always say, "we'll get to later." The fewer stacks that collect around your home and office, the better you will feel. While files on your computer still need to be maintained and organized, it's much easier to periodically go through computer files than it is to go through physical filing cabinets or drawers. Digital file storage also relieves you of the burden of physically searching for important papers or documents. Wherever you have access to your phone or computer, you will have access to all of your important papers. And if you keep your computer well-organized, you'll never have to frantically hunt for the document that you need.

Chapter 8: Dealing with Stress in Real Life

No matter what your stressors are, the daily relaxation technique that you choose will help you to cultivate a calm state of mind so that your overall stress levels stay at a healthy and manageable level. However, if you experience chronic stress, then your body and brain have probably developed some automatic coping mechanisms, ones that aren't necessarily going to disappear when you start your relaxation practice. Unhealthy coping mechanisms are emotional habits. They're automatic and unconscious reactions that we experience when faced with certain situations. Slowly but surely, you can begin to retrain your brain away from these coping mechanisms. Everyone develops slightly different coping mechanisms to help them manage chronic stress, but there are certain coping mechanisms that are more common than others.

Anger

Perhaps the most common coping mechanism people develop when faced with stressful situations is anger. Whether you scream and honk at other drivers on the road or see red whenever your child refuses to listen, anger is not always something you can prevent or control. It's a feeling like any other, and when it wells up, trying to pretend that you don't feel as angry as you do will only lead to more problems.

Anger is essentially a fear response. It's the "fight" half of the "fight-or-flight" instinct our bodies experience when confronted with danger. So when the body enters the stress response, your temper becomes a lot shorter. When you're stressed, you become angry far more easily than you do when you're relaxed. While anger can be justified, and sometimes healthy when you are truly in a hostile situation, flying into a rage at home or snapping at your coworkers never makes a situation better. Instead, anger often causes us to lash out at others in ways that we regret later. Instead of protection from harm, anger often creates an even worse situation.

When you become angry, irritable, or even just frustrated, there are a few things you can do to calm yourself down and not allow your feelings to overwhelm you. The first and most important thing to do when you get angry is to *think before you speak*. Anger can make us say some pretty nasty comments in the heat of the moment, and cause serious damage to our relationships. Whenever you get angry, commit to taking one deep breath before you say anything out loud. Do this every time you're called to speak until you feel your anger start to recede. The few seconds it takes to take one deep breath can stop us from saying something that could potentially cause years of damage to a relationship. This technique also has the added benefit of more deep breathing, a tried-and-true relaxation technique for any situation (Mayo Clinic Staff, 2020, "Anger...").

Another important anger management step is to *name your feelings*. When you keep your anger under control like this you do not try to deny it or hide it. If you feel angry or irritated, tell the other person in a respectful and honest way. Express your feelings to someone else in a way that isn't hurtful or confrontational. Simply say to the other person, "It makes me angry when you say this," or, "I'm just tired right now and little things are annoying me. Can we talk about this tomorrow?" These statements can go a long way toward conflict management. Anger is a defense response, and so in the heat of the moment, it's hard to imagine that the other person might not realize how angry or frustrated you are. Name your feelings honestly and respectfully to help you and your partner communicate without a fight (Mayo Clinic Staff, 2020, "Anger...").

Remember that you are never obligated to remain in situations where you feel hurt, threatened, or unsafe. If you have a surge of anger, don't be afraid to *remove yourself from the situation*. Leave the room or the conversation and take a few minutes by yourself to cool down and think more clearly. It is extremely difficult to calm yourself down when you are in the midst of a conflict. The anger response was triggered within you because you felt unsafe, and it will be nearly impossible for you to release that anger while you still feel like you are under attack. Remove yourself from the situation to regain a sense of safety. If you then have to revisit the situation that made you feel angry, then you can do so from a calm and secure state of mind (Mayo Clinic Staff, 2020, "Anger...").

Dealing with Difficult People

No relationship is perfect. But some can be bad more often than they can be good. These relationships, whether with friends, family, or coworkers, can become strained or even toxic. You can recognize a strained relationship if you begin to dread spending time with someone or if you always seem to end up in conflict. In place of these, you need to cultivate more positive and supportive relationships as a necessary part of your health and wellbeing. The stress and emotional exhaustion of negative relationships can actually be detrimental to your physical health. The straightforward answer when faced with a difficult person is to minimize your contact with them as much as possible. But what do you do when the difficult person in your life is a family member, co-worker, or another person that you can't simply stop speaking to?

As much as possible, *keep conversations neutral* with people that you find difficult or a challenge to be around. Avoid topics that are extremely personal or important to you. Reserve those conversations for people who bring you joy, and the people that you really love to be around. With difficult people, try to stay away from topics that are extremely divisive, like religion or politics - especially if either one of you has strong opinions on the matter. You don't have to agree with everyone. To avoid a conversation that will lead to an unhelpful argument is not cowardice - it is simply common sense. If the other person tries to engage you in a sensitive conversation, don't be afraid to change the subject. If they persist or become aggressive with you, leave the conversation entirely. It is helpful to remain open to outside ideas, but you are in no way obligated to have a conversation that you know will distress you.

Perhaps one of the hardest aspects of dealing with a difficult person is needing to *accept them for who they are*. You can't change the other person, and there's never a situation in which it's acceptable to try. No matter how good or justified your intentions are, an attempt to force another person to be someone or something that they're not is not "support" - it creates a power struggle. The attempt to change another person will cause them instead to become defensive and feel criticized. It is very difficult to get someone to listen to you if they feel that you're overly critical. In this scenario, ultimately *you* have become the source of the conflict. If you don't like who or what someone is, try to ask them questions to help you better understand what makes them the way that they are. We all contain multitudes.

You are also never obligated to give up your power to someone else - *control what you can control.* You can't change someone else's behavior, but you can always change the way that you respond to that behavior. If someone does something that you don't like, speak up. You don't have to respond with anger or aggressiveness, but be firm. If someone has treated you in a way that makes you feel unhappy, let them know in a respectful and honest way. If they continue to behave in an unacceptable manner, remove yourself from the conversation.

No matter how unjustified another person's behavior may seem, the fact of the matter is that most difficult relationships are created by a toxic dynamic that occurs between two people. Unless you are in an abusive situation, there is probably something you could do differently to improve the quality of your relationship. Again, this comes down to an examination of the ways that you respond to the behavior of others.

Whenever you find yourself engaged in conflict with a difficult person, take a mental step back. Is there something you could have done or said differently to avoid that conflict? The next time you are forced to spend time with this person, try to intentionally change the way that you respond to their difficult behavior. You may be surprised by how much a change in your reactions can improve the quality of your conversation. We sometimes don't realize how we come across to other people. You may unconsciously do something to make the other person feel hurt or defensive. While it never gives someone else the right to hurt or mistreat you back, it is important to take responsibility and at least make an effort to *create healthier patterns of communication* with this other person.

Something to keep in mind is that nobody in the world is completely "good" or completely "bad." When you engage with a difficult person, try to *focus on their positive qualities*. There is probably at least one quality about this other person that you can find to respect or admire. Focus on that one quality whenever you have to spend time with this person. Think about what you like about this other person instead of what you dislike and change the way that you engage with them. Your demeanor will be a lot less hostile. Almost always, the other person will respond positively to the change in your energy.

That being said, it is also important to *see the other person for who they are*. If you hate the fact that one of your friends can't keep a secret, then don't confide in them anymore. If your sibling constantly flakes out on you, then make less plans with them or rely on them for important commitments. Part of being able to accept someone for who they are is an acceptance of their negative traits. If someone is chronically unable to give you the affection you need, then it might be time to look for that affection elsewhere. Don't stubbornly try to force the other person to take on a role that you've assigned to them. That isn't fair to them or fair to you.

Assertive - To Be or Not to Be?

Assertiveness is a personality trait. Some people are naturally more assertive than others, and there's nothing immediately wrong with that. If you are a very assertive person, then you probably find it easy to fight for what you want. You may also be a straightforward communicator, unafraid of conflict, and find it easy to lay healthy boundaries in your relationships. However, not every situation calls for assertiveness. Sometimes being too assertive can create conflict, and that, in turn, creates stress. People might interpret your assertiveness as aggression, arrogance, or condescension. It's always good to be clear and honest about your needs and opinions. But depending on the social climate, it is sometimes advisable to let little things go or be a little more gentle.

Not every battle is worth the fight. Sometimes the people around us make mistakes. Sometimes people don't realize that they have hurt or inconvenienced us. Clear and honest communication is always good, but check your intensity. If you find it consistently difficult to get along with coworkers or constantly fight with your partner's family, take a mental step back. Is there a way that you could be a little more gentle or easygoing? Is there something about your communication style that causes the people around you to feel defensive or criticized?

On the other hand, not being assertive enough can also lead to stress. Not being able to clearly express or stand up for yourself can lead to a feeling of powerlessness and keep you from the things that you need out of life. People who are not naturally assertive tend to be more intuitive, gentle, and easygoing. You might find it easier to get along with people, and you may have good instincts when it comes to reading other people's feelings. Not being assertive certainly doesn't make you a pushover or a coward. Have you ever heard the saying, "You catch more flies with honey than with vinegar?"

Of course, certain people or situations in your life may sometimes call for a little vinegar. It is always okay to say "no" to requests that make you uncomfortable or to requests that will overburden you. It is also always okay to speak up if you feel angry or distressed. No one can read your mind. Often, others don't realize that the requests they make, or the way that they behave, causes you stress. The only way they will know is if you communicate clearly how you feel.

No matter what your situation may be, assertiveness is at the core of nearly every stressful situation. Whether in work, finances, or relationships, it is almost always a guarantee that if you feel stressed, then a state of assertiveness is part of the problem. Take a look at the situations in your life that stress you out. Are you too assertive in them, or are you not assertive enough? If you're not sure, it's okay to experiment. The next time you face a stressful situation, speak up. Lay stronger boundaries. Initiate conversations. See how the people around you react. Did your increase in assertiveness make the situation better? Or did it lead to more conflict?

Assertiveness is an especially important problem for people who experience stress in the workplace. Work-related stress is often interpersonal, even if it doesn't seem so on the surface. Even stressors such as low salaries, excessive workloads, or limited growth opportunities, are almost always rooted in how you interact with other people. If your salary is too low, have you asked for a raise? If your workload is more than you can handle, have you spoken to your boss or tried to delegate tasks out to other people? Are you saying "yes" to new assignments when you should be saying "no"? These situations might feel like they are totally out of your control, but it may really be the case that you are just not assertive enough. Asking for greater compensation for your role, or communicating to a superior that you feel overworked, are absolutely normal and acceptable parts of business communications. Any workplace that makes you feel like these ideas are not okay to say is not a healthy one. If you are underpaid or overworked (or both) and your boss doesn't want to acknowledge it, then it might be time to find another job.

However, work-related stressors can sometimes come from being a little *too* assertive. Your salary might be low, but are other people with your role paid a similar wage? It is always okay to negotiate for more money, but if your boss is not willing to increase your salary, it might not necessarily be because they undervalue you. If you already make a reasonable wage for your job and skill set, then a push for more money may create more stress and strain than it resolves. If you spend all of your energy on feelings of anger, or a sense of being undervalued, then you will further your stress and frustration. This can stop you from finding opportunities to increase your value in the workplace - and the option to argue for greater compensation in the future. No matter what causes you frustration at work, take a mental step back from the situation. Is this battle worth the fight? Is this situation worth the anger? Is there a way I can creatively solve this problem? Is this something that I simply need to let go of so that I can better enjoy other parts of my job and my life?

Chapter 9: Seven Examples of Stressful Events - Explained

Any situation can become a stressor depending on how you feel and react to it. However, there are seven major life events that are considered by psychologists to be the most likely to cause severe stress, both during, and long after an event has been resolved. Almost every individual will experience at least one of these events throughout their life, but it can be quite difficult to learn how to cope. Fortunately, there are many ways to handle the stress of these major events that are simple and grounding, ways that don't require much preparation or change to your already changing life.

Losing a Loved One

Perhaps the most stressful experience you can go through is the death of a loved one. Whether that person is a child, parent, family member, friend, or partner - grief is a very deep and often very traumatic experience. Everyone experiences grief differently. You may experience intense emotions like shock or anger. Other people experience feelings of guilt, depression, or even denial. While the intense feelings that come with grief are natural, they can later develop into trauma and long-term stress if they are not managed in a healthy way.

How to Manage the Stress of Losing a Loved One:

Perhaps the most important step you can take after losing a loved one is to *acknowledge your feelings*. Whether you feel shock, anger, or sadness, if you try to ignore or bury your feelings, it won't make them go away. If anything, it is the actual attempt to deny one's feelings that causes them to emerge later in life as chronic stress or deep-seated trauma. If you bottle up your feelings, you will place physical stress on the body, and create a great deal of psychological stress as you try to deny the truth of how you feel. If you have experienced the death of a loved one it is very important to be active and label your feelings, especially within the first three months. A mood chart is a useful tool to help name your feelings, and gives you more nuanced options than "good" or "bad," "happy" or "sad."

It is very important to accept that the emotions triggered by grief can be quite intense. Extreme emotions of anger or sadness are completely normal, and even healthy responses to grief. The loss of a loved one is a traumatic experience. Extreme emotions are your body's way of telling you that something terrible has happened. Acknowledging your feelings is a key part of this process. If you can acknowledge that you feel angry or depressed, then these surges of emotion won't take you by surprise. You won't be able to process your intense feelings in a healthy way if you can't even admit that you experience them. There is no shame in intense emotions, and there is no such thing as "too much" grieving, or an "overreaction" to the loss of a loved one.

Finally, remember that your grieving process will be unique to you. There is a common psychological grief scale developed in the 1960s called the Five Stages of Grief, which has helped many people to identify how they feel when faced with loss (Holland, 2018). The Five Stages of Grief are:

1. Denial
2. Anger
3. Bargaining
4. Depression
5. Acceptance

If in grief, use these five stages to better understand how you feel in the moment. Don't expect to move through the stages in the order that they are listed, and don't expect that you will experience every single stage. Everybody's grieving process is unique. Some people only experience two or three of the five stages. Some people experience depression before they experience anger, or even repeat stages that they have already experienced (Holland, 2018). There is no right or wrong way to grieve. The most important way to protect your body from even more stress is to know and accept where you are in the grieving process right now.

Major Illness or Injury

The diagnosis of a major illness or a severe injury can put much stress on the body. All of your body's resources will be devoted to healing the damage that has been done, whether that means fighting off an infection, managing a genetic condition, or repairing broken bones and tissues. Stress by itself can manifest as physical symptoms in the body, and so the stress sustained from a major illness or injury can make your experience much worse. Stress can prevent you from healing properly, cause you experience regressions, and put psychological problems on top of your physical ones.

How to Manage the Stress of Major Illness or Injury:

One of the biggest causes of stress that come from physical healing is uncertainty. Whether you've been diagnosed with an incurable condition or been in a severe car accident, what you will probably worry about most is the future. Will I be alright? Will I be able to return to my job or my passion? How will this affect my relationships? My family? The stress of not knowing what the future will hold is the most psychologically detrimental, one that can cause severe emotional distress if not managed in a healthy way. While there is no way to know the future for certain, *setting goals for therapy and rehabilitation* is a healthy way to plan for the future. Rather than a spiral down into endless worries about how to return to work or how much of a burden you will be on your partner, you can focus on the next step in your recovery. Set actionable goals for your recovery in order to give you something positive and productive to work toward. Enlist your family, friends, and doctors to help you to create and complete your recovery goals. This will also make you feel loved and cared for in a time that may be very painful or frightening, and will give your loved ones concrete ways in which they can support you.

If you focus on the outcome of your recovery goals, you will be better prepared to accept the changes that the illness or injury may make to your life. You can then adjust your lifestyle accordingly in small, actionable steps. Illness and injury can make us feel extremely powerless, and that powerlessness can also lead to extreme feelings of stress, fear, and anxiety. Focus on and achieve your recovery goals as a way to regain autonomy over your life. Complete these goals to fill you with much-needed confidence, and ensure that the additional physical symptoms of stress don't add to the pain you already experience.

Divorcing or Separating

Whether you need to divorce your married partner or separate from a long-term and intimate romantic partnership, the pain of separation can be so severe that many psychologists categorize it as a kind of grief. Your partner has not died, but in many ways you may feel as though you've lost them. You certainly may lose a relationship that once made you feel happy and secure. While they can also be positive experiences, often separations are angry or bitter, adding additional feelings of hurt, sadness, and pain to an experience that's already life-changing.

How to Manage the Stress of Divorcing or Separating:

View the end of your relationship as a loss that you need to grieve. Expect that you will experience a variety of intense emotions, and remember that these emotions are absolutely normal, common, and okay to feel. It doesn't matter if you have dated someone for three months or been married for ten years. There is no acceptable scale or timetable for the pain of separation, and, much like grief, there is no such thing as an "overreaction" to a separation. However, in the particular case of separation, the intensity of our feelings can sometimes lead us to do or say hurtful things to our former partner. Not only is this not a healthy way to process your own feelings, but it can make the situation between you and your ex-partner far more hostile. As such, *labeling your feelings* is an extremely important strategy for relieving stress and pain in a healthy way. This strategy is common to many stress management techniques, and we have written about this in a variation previously. If you try to ignore or dismiss your feelings, they can sometimes lead to an explosion outwards, which would cause you to do or say things that you would never normally do. All of your personal feelings are justified, but you cannot justify actions that are intentionally hurtful towards your partner. Even peaceful separations are painful. If you deny your feelings, you often make your situation worse. Name and accept the intensity of your emotions. Recognize them as a natural and healthy response to the pain of separation. Open, honest communication with your ex-partner is always a good idea, but during this process, don't try to confide or seek emotional support from them. This is a time instead to lean on the shoulder of a good friend or family member.

It is also important to be gentle with yourself during and immediately after the separation. Don't expect that you will perform as well at your job or keep up as efficiently with your household duties. Give yourself permission to take a break, and give yourself the space you need to heal from your loss. If you need some time to be alone, take it. If you need help to meet a deadline or complete a task that you would normally have been able to handle by yourself, don't be afraid to ask your loved ones for support. Remember that your ex-partner was not the only meaningful connection in your life. Reach out to family, friends, and even coworkers for a little extra support during your grieving period.

Financial Difficulties

Whether you experience a sudden loss of income or incur new major expenses like student loans, medical bills, or an increase in rent - financial difficulties can be an extreme source of stress. Concerns about the money that you need to pay your bills and support yourself can have serious consequences for your health. That stress only increases if other people are dependent on you for their security. Financial distress is increasingly common, and will soon become the number one cause of stress in the United States today. You are not alone.

How to Manage the Stress of Financial Difficulties:

Finances rarely affect just one area of your life. Your bills could cover: rent or mortgage, credit cards, medical, food, utilities, or even transportation. These often directly relate to your feelings of security in the home, as is the case with rent and utilities. If you have to scramble to pay one bill, it can often lead to a slippery slope of quick fixes and bad financial coping strategies that cause you even more stress and financial troubles down the road. The best way to cope with the stress that comes from financial strain is to *make one financial decision at a time*. Another way to think about this is to find one solution at a time. Don't all at once try to work more hours at your current job, take on a second (or third) job, ask your parents for help, and take out a new credit card. Don't make multiple changes to your finances all at one time, either. If you try to pay off your credit cards, save for retirement, and put your kids through college all at the same time, you will be left completely overwhelmed. Make one major financial goal your primary focus, and then manage the rest.

I understand that when you feel like you're drowning, this can be difficult advice to follow. But if you choose to focus on one item at a time, it will improve your ability to problem-solve. Instead of a constant scramble between items, make one financial goal your top priority. This will relieve stress and prevent you from making sudden, impulsive decisions out of fear or desperation. Determine what your number one financial priority is. Is it making enough to pay rent? Paying off your credit card debt? Getting ahead of your mortgage? Whatever it is, focus all of your efforts on solving that single problem. If paying off your mortgage is your most important goal, reorient your budget and financial habits around it. Pay the minimums on other bills like credit cards. Invest the minimum amount into your retirement fund or savings account. Tackle the most important problem first, and afterwards, you will find it easier to tackle your other financial prospects.

Losing a Job

Losing a job can be stressful for financial reasons, but it can also be a source of extreme emotional distress. Losing a job can lead to feelings of rejection, inadequacy, and low self-esteem. Regardless of the reason, many people feel shame, worthlessness, or even guilt after losing a job, especially if someone else is dependent on them. This can create some obvious financial stress, but it can also create stress in terms of our identities and social wellbeing. For many people, what they do for work is an important part of their identity, and so losing a job can negatively impact the way that they see themselves. Jobs can also be important social outlets, ones that might be cut-off or damaged.

How to Manage the Stress of Losing a Job:

No matter how you feel about your job, losing it will always be difficult. Not only have you lost a source of financial stability, but you have also potentially lost a feeling of control over your life, a professional identity, and self-esteem. Your self-confidence may take a hit, and your daily routine is greatly affected, leaving you with empty hours in your day. If your job was a social outlet or if one of your coworkers developed into a real friend, then you may also experience a loss of meaningful social connections. Perhaps most significantly, losing a job means a loss of security, for you and for your family.

So treat it as a proper loss, and *allow yourself to grieve*. Treat the loss of your job the same way that you would treat any other kind of loss. Accept the intensity of your feelings. Be proactive and label your emotions. Understand that strong feelings are completely normal. Reach out to your loved ones for emotional support, and be honest about your emotional needs. Most importantly, don't put pressure on yourself to go out and get a new job right away. This can be difficult advice to follow, especially if you face extreme financial pressure. But if you insist to yourself that you have to get another job as soon as possible, you will put an enormous amount of additional stress on yourself that you don't need. You are already under a lot of stress. Give yourself a few days to grieve, and when you jump back into the professional marketplace, put healthy limits on the amount of time and effort you put into the job search.

Having a Child

A new baby can be a great joy. However, a child can also be an extreme source of stress. A child represents new responsibilities, a number of different lifestyle changes, and new financial concerns. It is a lot of work to care for a child, and even when you're away, it will still be on your mind. Many people try to hide or downplay the stress they feel after the birth of a new child because of a feeling of shame or embarrassment. But that stress does not make you a bad or unloving parent. It is perfectly normal, common, and natural to feel overwhelmed by the responsibilities of a new life, no matter how many children you may already have.

How to Manage the Stress of Having a Child:

There are many different reasons why the arrival of a new child can be stressful, but one of the biggest sources of stress actually comes from the change in routine. The presence of a new member in your household radically changes your daily routine. There is suddenly a lot more that has to be done, and you probably feel as though you have less time to do it all. Worse, these new items are pushed to the top of your list. You can't reschedule or delegate your child, and often, you can't predict what your child will need from day to day. While you scramble to find a way to efficiently manage your time, it is very important to *set aside time for yourself*. Many parents find that the best time for this is just after the child (or children) have gone to sleep, but you can schedule this at any time that works for you and your family. Give yourself an hour every day to do something that you enjoy: take a bath, read a book, or watch TV. The amount of energy and time required to be a new parent makes relaxation time and self-care extra important. Without it, you will quickly burn out, and your stress symptoms will get worse and worse. If an hour for yourself means putting off housework or social obligations, then so be it. At this point in your life, taking care of yourself is just as important as taking care of your new baby. You need to be balanced in order to best help the others that rely on you.

Retirement

Believe it or not, retirement can be one of the most stressful events a person will experience in their lifetime. Many people spend the second half of their lives dreaming about their retirement, but are totally unprepared for the stress that accompanies it. This doesn't mean that your retirement will not be as wonderful as you planned. But retirement is a major life change, and like all major life changes, it comes with a fair amount of stress. What makes retirement particularly stressful is often the lack of preparation for that change.

How to Manage the Stress of Retirement:

One of the main reasons that retirement is so stressful is the change it makes to your identity. For many people, their career plays a major role in how they define themselves and how they relate to others. A job can define that part of yourself and how you live your life for decades. When that suddenly ends, it can create a kind of identity crisis. As a new retiree, you now have to rethink who you are and how you want to live your life. While that can be an exciting opportunity, it can also be extremely frightening.

The best way to avoid this sudden crisis of identity is to *retire slowly*. In the years before you plan to officially retire, try to reduce your hours or work part-time. This will give you more time to plan your life post-retirement, while simultaneously relieving the stress that comes with a 40 hour workweek. After a year or two of a reduced schedule, you will be comfortable and secure enough to officially end your career and start your new life as a relaxed retiree.

A slow retirement also gives you time to put your finances in order. Saving for retirement is something that most people only start to think about in middle age, so that they have enough to live on when they leave work. However, financial stability can be difficult (and stressful) to maintain even when you are at the peak of your career. Even the best planners can find themselves with unforeseen costs as retirement looms closer. Don't wait until retirement to learn that you don't have enough to cover your medical bills, or to live your preferred comfortable life. Instead, take the year or two prior to focus and go over your finances. You can then determine what adjustments will need to be made to ensure your financial security when you officially leave work.

Chapter 10: The Seven Habits of Good Stress Managers - Explained

All of the advice, techniques, and suggestions offered in this book can be grouped into seven major categories. Remember, these habits all take time to form, so don't expect to master them overnight. However, if you introduce any of these habits into your daily life, you will not only decrease your future stress levels, but you will also help your body to recover and heal from the damage done by living with stress in the past.

Knowing How to Relax

Your daily relaxation time may only be 5-15 minutes, but it will help you to feel calm and relaxed for hours afterward. Relaxation sounds like something you should be able to do automatically, but it is actually a habit you need to learn. It is something that you need to learn and practice every day, and it will take some time before it starts to feel comfortable or natural. According to a Wall Street Journal study, about 25% of their participants could be classified as workaholics, and 3% of their participants actually reported feeling physically ill when they tried to relax on vacation (Pinola, 2014). Our reactions to stress are learned habits as well, and it will take some time for you to unlearn those - in order to replace them with what your body and mind need to fully unwind.

Use your stress journal to help teach yourself what works for you and what doesn't. Take time to reflect on your relaxation techniques, record your stress levels every day, and keep track of your stressors. Whatever you determined your major stressors to be at the beginning of this book should be your main focus. Employ any strategy you can to relieve stress from those areas of your life. Make a note of how you feel in special situations or with people that stress you out. Return to those notes after you start your daily relaxation practice. Do you notice a change in your stress levels? Are you finding solutions to problems that you once thought were inevitable or unavoidable?

There is no one right or wrong way to relax. Some people find a great deal of stress relief from yoga, but it makes other people feel self-conscious, tired, or frustrated. Many people prefer the mental health benefits of meditation, but many others struggle with the practice. The key isn't just to relax, it is to know what works for you. If something causes difficulty for you, then don't feel obligated to keep at it. You should spend as much time thinking about your unique relaxation signature as you do your unique stress signature. We learned about stress signatures back in Chapter 3 - what are your stressors and what are your symptoms. Now, what kinds of situations, stimuli, or actions will make you feel relaxed? The more specifically you can answer that question, the better you will build your relaxation habit. Ultimately, it will become strong enough to counter your stress habits.

Eating and Exercising Correctly

It can't be overstated just how beneficial healthy eating and regular exercise is for the body. More nerves connect your brain to your gut than to any other organ in the body. The food that you eat affects everything from your energy levels to your mood to your body's ability to fight off disease. Thousands of studies have shown how healthy eating and exercise can be even more effective than prescription drugs to treat everything from cancer to diabetes to stress. You could consider an unbalanced diet a stressor simply because of the negative ways that it affects the body.

So, what does it actually mean to eat and exercise "correctly?" Should you go on a special diet? Should you count calories? What kind of exercises are best? There is so much information out there that it is difficult to know what works best for, especially when much of that information is conflicting. The best thing to do, always, is to listen to your body. If less carbs makes you feel better, then eat less and find substitutes. But if cutting carbs makes you sick, then keep incorporating them into your diet. Only you can know what routine works best for you, but I find that there is one single, simple dietary change with the greatest benefit and stress management impact.

Eat breakfast. Not necessarily a huge breakfast. But it is important to have something within a few hours of waking up. Many people count morning coffee as breakfast, but while coffee can give your brain a bit of a boost, it doesn't nourish your body with the nutrients it needs to thrive. On the other hand, many people also choose sweet or fatty comfort foods in the morning, like pancakes, bacon and eggs, or pastries. While these foods are tasty, they are also loaded with trans fats and sugars, which can even be worse than eating nothing at all. Whole-grain cereals, bread, low-fat milk, juice, a banana, yogurt, or pancakes are all great breakfast options. These options provide you with macronutrients (carbs, proteins, and healthy fats) that give your body the energy it needs to get you going in the morning. These meals are also packed with micronutrients, which are the vitamins and minerals that provide your body with nutrition.

Sleep Well and Enough

Sleep problems plague people who deal with chronic stress. Insomnia is a very common stress symptom, but insomnia itself can be a stressor, sending those with sleep problems into a vicious cycle of stress-related insomnia and insomnia-related stress. It is recommended that you get between seven and nine hours of sleep every night, but some people need a little less and others need a little more. But where many people get stuck is not the amount of time they spend asleep, but the quality of the sleep itself. Laying in your bed staring at the ceiling for seven hours is not the same as a full-night's sleep. Your sleep quality diminishes if you toss and turn, wake up repeatedly, or experience night terrors. Even if you manage to stay asleep for a full eight hours, if the overall quality of that sleep wasn't good, then it can still contribute to health problems in the brain and body.

A daily relaxation habit will naturally improve the quality of your sleep. If you're someone who struggles with insomnia, then you may want to consider a schedule with relaxation time just before you go to bed. But no matter when you've chosen to build your relaxation habit, it is always important to be screen-free for at least fifteen minutes before you go to bed. Smartphones, tablets, laptops, and TVs all emit a shade of blue light that stimulates the brain. Your eyes may begin to droop while you scroll through your smartphone before bed, but the stimulation to your brain can make it difficult for you to fall into a deep, restful sleep. It is also advised not to do anything in your bed except sleep. Your meals, your work, and your TV habits should be kept in another room. When you get into your bed, you want your brain to automatically start to prepare for sleep. If your bed is a place where you engage in many stimulating activities, then it can become difficult for your brain and body to relax while you're there.

Managing Anger

After anxiety, anger is the most commonly experienced symptom of stress. Feelings of irritability, frustration, and rage can be extremely difficult to control, and can rise up at even the slightest provocation. Too often, we unleash our anger on other people in an attempt to release some of the emotional pressure that stress builds up inside us. Unfortunately, this almost always makes the situation worse, adds damaged personal relationships to your list of stressors, and makes your anger even more difficult to manage.

A great anger-management strategy is the use of "I" statements. It can be far too easy to lay blame and hurl hurtful words at others when we feel angry. If we use "I" statements, we instead produce more constructive comments and communicate our feelings in a clear and respectful way. Of course, not all anger is unwarranted. If someone says something hurtful or acts violently, anger is a normal and occasionally helpful response.

But no matter how justified our anger may be, it is still not okay to be hurtful or violent ourselves.

"I" statements are exactly what they sound like - statements that start with "I." Instead of saying something unhelpful ("You're so lazy, you never do anything to help around the house") try something more constructive ("I am upset that you left the table without offering to do the dishes"). Your "I" statement can take as many forms as you have feelings ("I feel really frustrated when you leave your dishes in the sink for me to clean"). Instead of laying blame and judgment on someone else, keep the conversation focused on you and your feelings.

Another powerful anger management strategy is empathy. If you find yourself in continuous conflict with the same person, try to imagine what is going on in their life. Why do they behave that way? Try to imagine how they feel when you shout or speak sarcastically. If you imagine the other person's perspective, it can help you to let go of your anger and lead you to positive solutions that you were not able to see during the conflict.

Time Organization

There is nothing more overwhelming than a busy schedule. The feeling of having too much to do can be a significant source of stress. If we juggle too many commitments, we often make mistakes or miss important details that leave us with even *more* work to do, which increases our stress even more. If you feel stressed, then it is critically important to take a look at how you manage your time. Most people with busy schedules say that there is nothing they can do, but if you give yourself a moment to pause, you will find that there is almost always a way to give yourself a little bit of time to breathe.

A very important factor of good time management is to set clear goals. Often, individuals are overwhelmed with commitments because they don't have a clear vision of what they want out of life. It is difficult to make positive lifestyle decisions without being sure of what kind of life you want to lead, or even worse, when you try to follow goals that have been given to you by someone else. If you ever feel totally overwhelmed, take a moment to answer this question in your stress journal: *If I could magically change one thing about my life, with just a snap of my fingers, what would it be?* The answer to that question will almost always be a major source of stress for you. Now take a look at your life. Is there anything that you can do to make that change a reality? You may not be able to snap your fingers and make your supervisor or your debt disappear, but there is probably something you can change to make those stressors less potent. If you have a bad relationship with your supervisor, maybe dedicate some time in the morning to look for a new job. Arrive at the office earlier so that you can get settled before they arrive. If you're swamped with debt, make it your primary goal to pay it off. Once you focus your attention on the achievement of one purpose, you will suddenly find it much easier to make positive time management decisions. When paying off debt becomes a goal rather than a wish, you'll find it much easier to say "no" to situations that would increase the debt, or make it more difficult to pay off. You might also find it easier to take on greater financial opportunities, or find more motivation at your current job. With a goal to work toward, it will be much easier for you to eliminate unnecessary obligations from your schedule. You will find yourself with more energy to complete the tasks that move you toward the achievement of your goal.

Filter Out the Unimportant Things

The more stress something causes us, the more we start to magnify its importance in our lives. In the grand scheme of your life, your job might just be an easy way to pay the bills. But if you feel overworked or find yourself in constant conflict with your coworkers, then your job will start to feel like it is taking over your life. Rather than put your effort into the opportunities that *are* important to you, you will find yourself consumed with a job that was never meant to be the center of your life.

Keep your stressors in perspective as an effective way to manage how much they bother you. If something or someone is not that important to you, then don't waste your valuable time and energy on it. Instead, pour that energy and time into the things that are valuable to you. Identify the most important people in your life, and put all of your efforts into the maintenance of those positive relationships. If your boss, or your mother-in-law, or your ex-boyfriend are not on that list of important people, then choose not to let them get to you. Find ways to keep conversation civil when difficult people are around, but don't waste your time and struggle to make it work when instead you could spend time with someone that you truly love.

Take a look at your skills and talents. What you're naturally good at often contains clues about what you truly value, or the situations that make you naturally feel secure. If you're really good at something obscure like marbles or ping pong, try to think about *why* you're so good at those games. Are you naturally dexterous? Do you enjoy healthy competition? Maybe you enjoy fine skill over brute force? This won't necessarily mean that you are destined to become a professional ping pong player, but whatever makes you successful at ping pong may also be a skill you can take to other parts of your life. It is healthy to seek things out that you are good at. You will feel more confident, and therefore more relaxed, if you seek out situations that allow your natural gifts to thrive.

Try Having Humor

Laughter truly is the best medicine. The ability to make people laugh will naturally make people feel more relaxed around you, and in turn, make you feel relaxed about them. If you can find the humor in a situation, no matter how stressful, then that will make it much more manageable. Laughter is also a natural way to release tension, and a much healthier method than anger. Finding the humor doesn't mean you will make light of a serious situation. It is just a way to keep things in perspective, and to help you face life with joy rather than tension.

Humor is a communication skill, and it is one that doesn't always come easy. Everyone has a slightly different sense of humor, and your sense of humor can even change slightly depending on who you're with. Not every situation is a laughing matter, and making a joke about a topic that the other person feels is insensitive can create greater tension, rather than diffusing it. Not everyone finds silly or raunchy humor amusing, and it is very easy to mishear sarcasm, especially if it comes from a stranger.

It can be complicated to keep all this in mind and make humor seem like a pretty risky endeavor, or even take the fun out of it. But don't let it stress you out. Humor should lessen your stress, not add to it. The trick with humor is not to worry about doing something silly or having a perfect clever quip. Instead, just think about ways to make the person in front of you smile! Laughter doesn't have to come from jokes or humor. It can come from something sweet, or pleasantly surprising. Make it your goal to make the person you're with smile, and you will almost certainly get a laugh from them as a bonus. Think about what will make the other person smile to help take your mind off of your own stress or feelings of awkwardness. It will help you to connect with that person on a closer level. And, of course, it always feels good to make someone else happy. Making other people smile and laugh is an almost instant stress reliever.

Conclusion

Every individual will experience stress at one point in their lives. That's honest, and that's okay. A little bit of stress can actually be good for us. It can give us an extra boost of energy when we lack motivation, or make us aware of problems that we couldn't see before.

Stress is built into our bodies as a natural response to danger. In many ways, stress is what keeps us alive. It alerts us to threats, and provides us with the energy and alertness that we need to successfully combat them.

However, when stress becomes chronic, then our bodies and minds are thrown out of balance. Just as we need a little bit of stress to thrive, we also need to relax. Without time to rest and recuperate from the stresses of life, our bodies become physically weakened and even ill. Our minds stop working as effectively. We find it more and more difficult to think clearly, regulate our moods, and even start to develop harmful psychological patterns or disorders.

You chose to read this book because you felt the harmful presence of chronic stress in your life. No matter how long you battled stress in the past, or how severe your stressors are, you now have all the tools you need to manage your stress in a healthy way that works uniquely for you. No two people's stress is identical. But you now have a clear understanding of what your stressors are and how they affect your body and mind. To understand your stressors is half the battle. With your stress journal in hand, you are now ready to take action to get your stress back under control.

Perhaps the most important technique outlined in this book is to schedule a daily relaxation time. Spend just five minutes a day on a deep breathing technique and watch it work wonders for your mental and physical health. Build from there. Don't reject a technique out of hand because it sounds simple. Stressful situations are often big and complex, and so we tend to feel that our solutions should be big and complex as well. But stress is the opposite of relaxation, in almost every way. It is often the case that the simplest of relaxation techniques has the greatest effect on the most complex life stressors.

As you start to apply the techniques outlined in this book, always remember to be patient with yourself. No technique will work immediately. Remember, stress is a habit too. Our stress responses often surprise us; they take over our thoughts and behaviors before we even realize what happened. The management of those automatic thoughts and feelings will take some time and practice. It may take you a while to find a relaxation technique that works well for you. You may also learn new sides to your stressors and your responses to them. Why do they stress you out the way they do? You might even realize that what you initially thought was a stressor was really just a distraction, and that there is another, truer source of stress to tackle. The more you learn about yourself, the more effective action you can take to manage your stress. You may even find yourself with the tools to eliminate your stressors altogether.

Stress has a unique ability to distort our situation, and make it look much worse than it actually is. No matter how terrible you feel, know that there is always something you can do to make the situation better. But before you can start to find a solution, you have to find a way to relax. We are naturally better problem-solvers when we're relaxed, as opposed to when we're stressed. Stress management can be a cure, but it can also be a prevention strategy. A daily relaxation habit is intended to help you feel relaxed all the time. Don't wait for moments of stress to practice your relaxation techniques. While there are many strategies in this book that you can employ in the moment to help you through a bad situation, these situational coping strategies are no match for a daily relaxation habit. Right now, your mind's natural state may be one of stress. Your automatic responses to new situations may be fear, anger, and frustration. But as you start to practice your daily relaxation technique, you will start to feel your perspective shift. Rather than fear or anxiety in new situations, you will instead find feelings of excitement, wonder, and curiosity. Rather than a rage response, you will instead calmly roll up your sleeves and resolve the sudden changes or challenges in front of you.

My hope for you is that, where once you felt overwhelmed, you now feel empowerment. You now have the tools you need to take back control of your mind, your feelings, and your life. And above all, you now have the ability now to feel good about yourself. I know that with time and patience, you will find relaxation techniques that work for you. Once you do - your life will transform for the better. You already took a huge first step by simply reading this book, so good luck on your journey! Know that there is at least one person out there rooting for you!

References

Albrecht, Karl. (1979). *Stress and the Manager.* New York, York: Simon & Schuster.

Avoiding Roadblocks to Stress Reduction. (2016, March 26). https://www.dummies.com/religion/spirituality/avoiding-roadblocks-to-stress-reduction/

Butler, G. (1993, August 1). Definitions of Stress. https://www.ncbi.nlm.nih.gov/pmc/articles/PMC2560943/

Davis, M., Eshelman, E. R., & McKay, M. (2008). *The Relaxation and Stress Reduction Workbook*. New York, New York: New Harbinger Publications.

Elkin, A. (2013). *Stress Management For Dummies*. Hoboken, NJ, United States: Wiley.

Figueroa-Frankhanel, Frances. (2014, December 12). Measurement of Stress. https://secure.jbs.elsevierhealth.com/action/cookieAbsent?code=null

Freeman L (2009). Relaxation therapy. In Mosby's Complementary and Alternative Medicine: A Research-Based Approach, 3rd ed., pp. 129–157. St. Louis: Mosby Elsevier.

Haas, S. (2017, September 30). 7 Ways to Calm Your Worried Mind and Reduce Anxiety. https://www.psychologytoday.com/us/blog/prescriptions-life/201709/7-ways-calm-your-worried-mind-and-reduce-anxiety

Holland, K. (2018, September 25). What You Should Know About the Stages of Grief. https://www.healthline.com/health/stages-of-grief

Kunos, G., and Ciriello, J. (1992). *Central Neural Mechanisms in Cardiovascular Regulation, Vol. 2*. Boston, Birkhauser.

Lazarus, R.S., and Folkman, S. (1984). *Stress, Appraisal and Coping.* New York, Springer.

Lazarus, R.S., and Holroyd K.A. (1982). *Stress, Coping and Somatic Adaptation.* New York, Springer.

Legg, Timothy. (2020, March 29). Causes of Stress: Recognizing and Managing Your Stressors. https://www.healthline.com/health/stress-causes

Manage Your Stress: A Three-Pronged Approach. (2016, March 26). https://www.dummies.com/health/mental-health/stress-management/manage-your-stress-a-three-pronged-approach/

Mayo Clinic Staff. (2020, February 29). Anger Management: 10 Tips to Tame Your Anger. https://www.mayoclinic.org/healthy-lifestyle/adult-health/in-depth/anger-management/art-20045434

Mayo Clinic Staff. (2020, April 18). Relaxation Techniques: Try These Steps to Reduce Stress. https://www.mayoclinic.org/healthy-lifestyle/stress-management/in-depth/relaxation-technique/art-20045368

NHS Inform. (2020, April 24). Relaxation Techniques. https://www.nhsinform.scot/healthy-living/preventing-falls/fear-and-anxiety-about-falling/relaxation-techniques

Pinola, M. (2014, March 20). How You Can Learn to Finally, Really Relax. https://lifehacker.com/how-you-can-learn-to-finally-really-relax-1548045887

Puddicombe, A. (2011, January 24). How to meditate in 10 easy steps. https://www.theguardian.com/lifeandstyle/gallery/2011/jan/22/how-to-meditate-ten-steps-headspace

Scott, E. (2019, June 24). How to Get Organized to Manage Stress. https://www.verywellmind.com/tips-on-getting-organized-3145158

Scott, E. (2020, January 19). The Main Causes of Stress. https://www.verywellmind.com/what-are-the-main-causes-of-stress-3145063

Segal, J., Smith, M., Segal, R., and Robinson, L. (2020, April 16). Stress Symptoms, Signs, and Causes. https://www.helpguide.org/articles/stress/stress-symptoms-signs-and-causes.htm

Selye, H. (1956). *The Stress of Life.* New York, McGraw-Hill.

Seppala, Emma. (2019, November 7). Four Ways to Calm Your Mind in Stressful Times.

https://greatergood.berkeley.edu/article/item/four_ways_to_calm_your_mind_in_stressful_times

Stress Definitions from Stress Researchers. (2013, March 31). http://www.gostress.com/stress-definitions-from-stress-researchers/

Voltolina, V. (2017, September 22). 3 Easy Tricks to Get Organized and Reduce Stress. https://www.huffpost.com/entry/organization-and-stress_n_5851704?guccounter=1&guce_referrer=aHR0cHM6Ly93d3cuZ29vZ2xlLmNvbS8&guce_referrer_sig=AQAAAJwZSkH65kL_l4oait4Okd1wfo59-2sOzBBVGJYQH01iX2y9Hdx-gUONVDmi1tp3FM8xV4RzZn-wwP9jIXDi0XGXWltiz1BEatmSmCjSj3Hat-fbJEm48p-Xp6573f5JJSzpwvjU0Ovp47Yzp2ldngPjpOYTW2ffuV3ohwQwemB0

The Effective Relaxation Techniques

Learn How to Reduce Stress and Anxiety in Just 7 Days with Proven Relaxation Techniques

Nathan Golden

© Copyright 2020 - All rights reserved.

The content contained within this book may not be reproduced, duplicated or transmitted without direct written permission from the author or the publisher.

Under no circumstances will any blame or legal responsibility be held against the publisher, or author, for any damages, reparation, or monetary loss due to the information contained within this book, either directly or indirectly.

Legal Notice:

This book is copyright protected. It is only for personal use. You cannot amend, distribute, sell, use, quote or paraphrase any part, or the content within this book, without the consent of the author or publisher.

Disclaimer Notice:

Please note the information contained within this document is for educational and entertainment purposes only. All effort has been executed to present accurate, up to date, reliable, complete information. No warranties of any kind are declared or implied. Readers acknowledge that the author is not engaged in the rendering of legal, financial, medical or professional advice. The content within this book has been derived from various sources. Please consult a licensed professional before attempting any techniques outlined in this book.

By reading this document, the reader agrees that under no circumstances is the author responsible for any losses, direct or indirect, that are incurred as a result of the use of the information contained within this document, including, but not limited to, errors, omissions, or inaccuracies.

Your Free Relaxation Checklist!

(Ensure to take care of your well-being...)

This Checklist includes:

- Relaxation techniques you can do from home
- Stress Management timetable so you can organize your daily activities
- Progress monitorization log

The last we want is for your well-being to suffer because you weren't prepared.

To sign up and receive your survival checklist, click the link:

https://yourrelax53893.activehosted.com/f/3

We will send you an email shortly after you apply with details to download your checklist!

Introduction

"Set peace of mind as your highest goal, and organize your life around it." Brian Tracy

It's normal to experience stress. We all go through stressful situations at some point in our lives. These situations range from minor nuisances like traffic jams to more serious issues like losing your job or a loved one. When faced with these stressful situations, our bodies are flooded with emotions, our anxiety levels increase, our hearts beat faster and our muscles tense. Well, this is how the body responds to stress and anxiety. In fact, it's normal for the body to enter into a "fight or flight"(stress) response. It's a deep-rooted response that helps us to survive through threatening situations.

The truth is that we cannot avoid the diverse sources of stress that we're constantly exposed to. Nonetheless, we can choose healthier ways of responding to these stressors. One effective way of doing this is through "relaxation response." For most of us, relaxation means zoning out in front of our television sets or flopping on the couch at the end of a tiresome day. In reality, this does little to help us overcome stress and anxiety. Activating your body's natural stress response, on the contrary, puts your body in a state of deep rest. It is in this state that you can achieve peace of mind and relieve yourself from stress and anxious thoughts that are wearing you out.

Practicing relaxation techniques helps to quieten your mind. Your body and mind are brought to balance. There are different types of relaxation techniques that you can turn to. Some of these include deep breathing, yoga, rhythmic exercise, tai chi, meditation and so on. It's worth noting there is no single relaxation method that works for everyone, as we all have varying relaxation points. The way your body enters into a deep state of rest is different from how another individual would relax. This means that the right relaxation technique for you is one that resonates with you. Your ideal technique should be the one that can help your mind relax and evoke the relaxation response you direly need. More importantly, it should fit your lifestyle.

With the plethora of relaxation techniques available out there, you need to try these methods until you find the right one that suits you. It's then that you will continue practicing these relaxation techniques to ensure that you overcome everyday stress and anxiety. Ultimately, this will help boost your mood and energy, improve your sleep and enhance your overall health and wellbeing.

When stress gets the best of you, even the people who seem to be the strongest can find it daunting to find their Zen again. Worst, the emotional burden of stress builds up overtime. Unfortunately, this affects your life in every way. It robs you the joy of being in the present moment to enjoy life as it unfolds itself. It prevents you from experiencing growth through challenges. This happens because you will have a pessimistic outlook towards life.

Fortunately, you can learn to silence the outside world through the relaxation techniques that will be discussed and effectively described in this guide. Maybe you've been struggling to calm your mind and that it appears overwhelming because stress seems and anxiety seems to build up. The more you think about the challenges you might be going through, the more stressed and anxious you get. So, if you're going through a rocky relationship, a financial predicament, loss of a job, or that you're simply overthinking about your future, all these can greatly contribute to anxiety disorders.

In this guide, I am going to help you understand and master how to effectively use relaxation techniques to your advantage. I will take you through the different proven and tested techniques to help in calming the mind. It's through these lessons that you will be able to find your Zen again. Ultimately, through the peace of mind that you will achieve, you will organize your life around it.

Over the years, I have had the privilege and honor to help people overcome stress and anxiety. I have helped and transformed the lives of hundreds of people through counseling and workshops. Indeed, this has been a humbling experience. One thing that I have learned through the years is that individuals don't know how to relax. Most people are simply aware of simple relaxing techniques that might not be as effective when faced with overwhelming levels of stress and anxiety.

While working with different clients, all with varying reasons for stress and anxiety, I have garnered sufficient knowledge to realize that some relaxation techniques are more effective than others. This manual will, therefore, provide you with insightful information concerning the relaxation techniques that will work best for you. Remember, this book doesn't just stop there, it will also help you put these techniques into practice. I use these techniques on myself and my family and I can assure that this guide will significantly improve your well-being and that of the people around you.

Once you've mastered how to use the relaxation techniques in this book, you will notice your life transform in ways you've never imagined before. You will regain your self-confidence and you will live a more relaxed life. Since you will effectively manage your daily stressors, there is a good chance that you will live a life full of abundance. We often stress because we approach life with a pessimistic attitude, thinking about what we lack or worrying that everything is crumbling down on us. A change of attitude will free you from this mindset. You'll stop feeling the annoying chest heaviness that often accompanies overthinking.

People's testimonies on how their lives have changed through my guided relaxation techniques have been the main motivation behind writing this book. In this guide, I will take you through different forms of relaxation techniques that have helped most of my clients. Plus, I will also explain to you how certain lifestyle choices can help you reduce stress. Most importantly, I will highlight proven ways of relaxing through physical meditation exercises and socializing.

Some of the relaxation techniques in this manual only require a few minutes of your time. Others might take up to 20-30 minutes, but they will help you fine-tune your entire life. You can make this guide your best friend to help you ease or lower your levels of anxiety and stress. I highly recommend that you go through all the relaxation techniques so that you find one that serves you best.

You must have heard that "old habits die hard?" Well... it's true, especially when it comes to your health and well-being. Human brains are like a sponge, and over time our brain will fill up with old and bad habits that are daunting to change and overcome. So, it's very important for you to teach yourself how to overcome the stress and anxiety that you suffer from, or you will miss out on the most valuable times of your life.

Living a happy life demands that you combine effective relaxation techniques alongside an optimistic attitude towards life. This wisdom is within you. Honing your ingrained life skills requires that you learn to trust your intuition. This will help you leverage on your power to transform your life. The time to change is NOW.

Chapter 1: The Secrets of Reacting to Stress and Anxiety

Stress and anxiety are difficult to avoid these days. There are numerous things that compete for your time and attention every day: it's hard to avoid stress even when you are having a good day. You might have had a positive attitude about how your day will turn out, but if traffic jams prevent you from arriving at work on time, this might cause you to be stressed. One phone call with bad news from a friend could also affect how you feel about the entire day. The point here is that stress is part of everyday life. The only thing you can do to ensure that stress doesn't affect your outlook towards life is to learn how to cope with it healthily.

Before you learn how to cope with stress, the first thing that you should strive to understand is the sources of your stress. It is by understanding your sources of stress and anxiety that you will be better placed to know how to react differently. There is a huge difference between how successful people react to stress and how others do. For instance, successful people understand that life has its ups and downs. When things are not going their way, they use this opportunity to learn from their bitter experiences. On the contrary, when things seem to work out, they use the opportunity to transform their lives for the better.

Evaluating How You React to Stress

Managing stress and anxiety is not easy. It's also not difficult. The only thing is that the effects of stress and anxiety might fail to portray themselves like other forms of diseases. This means that it might take you some time to accept that you're suffering from stress and anxiety-related disorders. Most people end up treating themselves for the wrong diseases while the root cause of their health issues is stress and anxiety. This is even true for weight-related issues: sometimes life can seem overwhelming and it can negatively affect your food choices. We all know how difficult it is to hit the gym when your mind is not at peace. Going for the morning jogs you were used to could suddenly seem impossible.

At the end of the day, stress and anxiety prevent you from taking action. They stop you from living the life that you've always wanted to live, robbing you of living a joyous life.

To overcome stress and anxiety, your first steps should be to identify your sources of stress. The reasons why you're stressed are different from why your friend feels like their lives are not turning out like they should, so it's very important that you never equate yourself to another individual. Plus, you never know if someone can manage their stressors better than you. As such, assuming that you're sailing on the same boat might give you the wrong impression about how you feel about yourself and the people around you.

Unfortunately, stress and anxiety management skills don't come out as you might have expected. If we all knew how to cope with stress and anxiety, there would be no need for you to read this guide. Stress management skills can be learned; you can also polish your existing skills to improve on how you manage stress.

To understand how you deal or react with stress, take a moment to evaluate yourself. People are different. Some folks turn a blind eye on the daily stress triggers that surround them. We often perceive these people as strong as it appears as though they never get stressed. In reality, everybody gets stressed. The only difference is that some of us have admirable stress management skills. So, the idea that there is a tight deadline coming up would not be a reason to be anxious or stressed for some of us.

Other people have poor stress management techniques.

For example, at the first glimpse of a stressful situation, your anxiety levels surge. You're running late for a meeting and you can't stop thinking about the previous warning your boss gave you. This leads to incessant negative thoughts. Will I get fired? Maybe this will affect my promotion! Why did I snooze my alarm? All these thoughts fill your mind and make you panic. These negative thoughts influence your decisions. Since you're thinking negatively, there is a good chance that you will make the wrong decisions. Ultimately, you may find yourself in a vicious cycle of negative thinking.

If you're not sure about how you react to stress, monitor yourself for a week. Note down the stress triggers that make you anxious. Take this opportunity to also note down how you respond.

What happens when you're dealing with pressure or a tight deadline at work? Does this aggravate you to the extent that you release your anger on your fellow workers, friends or loved ones? When having a bad day at work, one may want to carry their bad temper at home. If your partner provokes you when you're feeling as though you should be left alone, you may lash out with harsh words at them. Realize that it has little or nothing to do with the stress you're going through.

Stress can also make you overreact. Instead of understanding that your partner made a small mistake, you may want to make a mountain out of a molehill.

This is something that many people in relationships struggle with. For instance, when going through a financial predicament, you could react if your partner spends money on something that you had not budgeted for. Sure, this is not the right thing to do. However, it's also not an excuse to pick a fight with your partner. There is a healthy way of responding to this to ensure that your relationship doesn't suffer under the strain.

Some people respond to stress by choosing to overeat. Research shows that stress can drive people to engage in "comfort eating." This is where people turn to foods that are high in sugar, calories, and fat (Jáuregui-Lobera & Montes-Martínez, 2020), leading to weight gain.

Chronic stress can also make you feel like there is too much to handle in your life. You may feel as though there is a lot of pressure from all corners. Your relationship is suffering, your career is on a downhill, and the people you call your friends might seem to care less. The truth is that your mind is suffering. Everything else around you is normal. If there is someone that needs to change, it's you.

Some people respond to stress by choosing to develop a negative mindset about everything. When you're stressed, this may have an impact on your perspective towards life and the people around you. For instance, instead of seeing good in things that happen around you, you may think differently. Even when good things are happening in your life, you may think that this will only last for a short time before something bad happens. Indeed, this is the worst way of responding to stress. As you might have guessed, it prevents you from seeing that life is full of abundance despite the challenges you're facing.

We also know of individuals who turn to drugs and alcohol when they are stressed. Studies reveal that there are millions of people who turn to alcohol and drugs when faced with stressful situations (Buddy T, 2016). Drinking might seem to provide you with some sense of relief. After a few glasses of whiskey, you may feel relaxed. However, it should be noted that this relief will only last for a short period. You won't have learned anything about managing your stressors or anxiety triggers. Worst, if your stress isn't taken care of, it could lead to overindulgence. This might lead to psychological and medical complications.

The way you react to stress has a huge impact on how you perceive your life and everything that is happening around you. But what causes you to be stressed or anxious in the first place? Let's look at some of the common stress and anxiety triggers.

The 4 Basic Sources of Stress and Anxiety

Studies reveal that there are approximately 33% of individuals who report feeling extremely stressed. The worst thing is that about 77% of people who feel stressed claim that it affects their physical health. 73% of individuals who suffer from stress claim that their mental health suffers a great deal (The Recovery Village, 2020).

In reality, there are many reasons why people suffer from stress. Depending on one's direction of thinking, anything can cause stress.

Take a moment to reflect on why you feel stressed today. Why are you in the position you are in today? What is it that you keep ruminating about? Maybe your financial situation is bothering you. It could be that your relationship is not turning out as expected or that you feel that you're not going anywhere with your partner. Your personal health issues might be the reason why you feel stressed. The family responsibilities on your shoulder could also make you feel stressed and overwhelmed. The point here is that there are numerous causes of stress. These causes can be categorized into 4 different sources.

Your Surrounding Environment

Stressors in your surroundings are termed as environmental stressors. These stressors can cause minor or major irritations in your everyday life. For instance, if you're working in a hot environment, the extreme temperatures can make you uncomfortable. The same case applies if you're working in a noisy environment. You may feel uncomfortable because your mind cannot think straight or you cannot hold a peaceful conversation with someone. Other environmental stressors include crowding, light, air quality, insects, war, tornadoes, and other natural disasters.

Your body reacts in a predictable manner when faced with a stressor. For instance, if you see a snake, your body will enter into the "fight-or-flight" response. The bodily response, in this case, is to "fight" the snake or "flight" - run away. This is what most people term as "adrenaline rush." Immediate threats like this example have less impact on your health as compared to long-term threats. If you keep experiencing a particular threat that makes you nervous from time to time, you may suffer the effects in the long run.

When your body enters the fight-or-flight response, it releases stress hormones such as norepinephrine and epinephrine. These chemicals are responsible for how your body responds when faced with a stressful situation. You may notice a sudden change in your heartbeat. Your palms could get sweaty and your hands could begin to shake. These physical changes are a result of the stress hormones that your body is releasing. It's important to understand that the frequent release of these hormones can affect your emotions. Your problem-solving ability will also be affected and you could even lose control of your bowels.

There are long term health effects that you could face if you constantly face environmental stressors that make your body enter into a fight or flight response. If you live in an environment prone to natural disasters, you're more likely to feel stressed or anxious. This happens because the stressors around you might be too much for the body's immune system to handle. Your blood sugar levels could spike up and you could face heart health issues. Frequent exposure to environmental stressors can contribute to mental health issues like anxiety, schizophrenia, and depression (Schimelpfening, 2015).

Social Stressors

The relationship with your social environment can also cause strain in your life. Social stress can include stress stemming from the struggles you go through at home, academic competition, friendship groups and so on. Even though social stress is not recognized as a major form of stress, it still ranks among the common forms of stress that people go through. One of the main causes of this type of stress is failure. Failure often leads to the loss of self-confidence and self-esteem. When one fails, they perceive themselves as though they have lost their social standing. Failure largely contributes to an increase in social stress because we live in a society where everybody yearns for approval. People usually characterize others based on how successful they are.

Another cause of social stress is the feeling of uncontrollability. Uncontrollability creates an environment where one feels like they have failed in life. It plants a seed of failure in the brain. When this happens, one feels paralyzed as they are unable to take desired actions in their lives that would lead to success. The effect of this is an increase in cortisol levels, a hormone responsible for helping you manage stress (Ana, 2018). In turn, the increase of cortisol levels in your body leads to decreased self-esteem.

If left untreated, the two causes of social stress will often lead to decreased self-esteem. This means that you will continue experiencing social stress and the effects are simply unbearable. When the brain is forced to frequently cope with social stressors, it releases several chemicals to help it cope with these stressful situations. Examples of these chemicals include dopamine, serotonin, and glutamate. When these chemicals are in present in the body in excessive amounts, it could lead to serious mental disorders (Ana, 2018). There are some physical illnesses which are caused by increased levels of social stress: certain cancers, ulcers, and cardiovascular disease.

So, how can you go about alleviating social stress? While there is no outright cure for it, there are a number of things that you can do to help yourself. An effective way of doing this starts with talking to the people that are close to you. If there are any broken relationships, fix them through regular communication. Indeed, we all know that there is power in sharing. A problem shared is a problem half solved. Talk to someone close to you about how you're feeling. This could help relieve some stress off your shoulders.

Another ideal way of dealing with social stress is by getting rid of toxic relationships. Toxic relationships are those relationships that negatively affect your mental and emotional state. Staying away from these relationships might help you improve your mental state.

While you can't "cure" social stress, the good news is that relief is attainable. The only thing you need to do is to open up and show that you're determined to relieve such stress in your life.

Physiological Stressors

Another source of stress that you may be experiencing is physiological. Just as the name suggests, this type of stressor relates to the physical aspects of your body. We cannot deny the fact that we are often stressed with our bodies. Many people will go to extremes to ensure that they lose weight or that their bodies look great. Statistics reveal that 62% of U.S. consumers who wish to eat a plant-based diet do to reduce weight. Only 17% of them do it to save money (Conway, 2018). Going by the numbers, this is a clear indication of what people are willing to do to ensure that they are physically fit.

As people grow older, they go through numerous physical changes. Sometimes these changes are difficult to cope with and thus, they could cause stress. For women, menopause brings a huge transition in their lives. Other triggers like lack of exercise, inadequate sleep, poor nutrition, aging, and injuries all tax the body. The manner in which you react to these changes can affect how you feel about yourself. If you think that you're gaining a lot of weight and there is little you're doing to remedy the situation, you may find yourself feeling stressed. If you continue going through the same feeling, it can take a huge toll in your life, leading to stressful symptoms like stomach upsets, muscle tension, anxiety, and headaches.

Your Thoughts

Have you ever stopped for a moment to consider the fact that everything you're thinking about is what you always attract into your life? In other words, you are the creator of your own little world. There are over 60, 000 thoughts that replay themselves in our minds daily. Experts believe that 90% of these thoughts are similar to what we were thinking about the previous day ("Destructive thinking: The hidden cause of stress," 2019). Interestingly, we can raise our awareness of these thoughts, but we often pay little attention to them.

The thoughts that replay themselves in our minds is what we call self-talk. When our minds replay these thoughts over and over, we begin to hold them to be true about ourselves. For instance, when your mind keeps telling you that you're wrong, chances are that you will always be skeptical about everything you do. How many times have you found yourself thinking,

"Why do I keep making the same mistakes?" This is a mistaken belief that has replayed in your mind until you started believing it was true. Breaking away from this thought cycle is integral to your mental health. It's important that you realize that you're not your thoughts. These are just random thoughts in your mind and they hold nothing on you. Raising your awareness about your thoughts will help in mastering how to quieten your mind. More about this will be discussed in the following chapters.

How Stress Works

Your thoughts are a major source of stress. To clearly understand how stress works with regards to your thoughts, psychologist Albert Ellis used a model called the ABC stress model. This model argues that external events (A) are not the reason for your emotions (C), but your beliefs (B) are to be blamed (Selva, 2018).

Another way of looking into this is that our behaviors and emotions (C) are not directly influenced by our life events. Rather, they are influenced by the way we cognitively process and evaluate (B) these events.

This model goes further to point out that the way we respond to stress is not an unchangeable process. The manner in which events lead to beliefs that lead to certain consequences is not fixed. The issue here is that the type of *belief* that we choose to hold on to matters the most. As human beings, we have the power to change what we choose to believe. For that reason, we can manage stress by accepting the rational beliefs we have and disputing the irrational beliefs that mislead us.

To put it simply, changing your negative self-talk to a more optimistic self-talk can change your negative beliefs. Positive self-talk can help you cope with the challenges you face in life.

Self-talk is the constant conversation that you have with your inner-self when no one is listening. Nobody can hear your self-talk apart from you. It's the voice of your thoughts speaking to you. There is power in these thoughts as they can make or break you. Positive self-talk will fill you with a positive mindset. It will fuel you to face life with courage. Negative self-talk, on the other hand, will aim to bring you down.

Once you become aware of your thoughts, you can learn to change your negative self-talk into positive. When faced with daily stressors, your mind can be filled with negative thoughts about the experiences you're going through. You might think that you're not perfect, that you have no control over your happiness, or that you cannot do it, or that asking for help is a sign of weakness, etc. Clearly, this is destructive thinking. You can change these thoughts by changing how you think. Ultimately, you will change how you respond to stress.

Behavioral Responses to Stress

Stress will affect your emotions. In turn, this means that your behavior will also change. Common behavioral symptoms that you will experience as a result of stress include changes in your appetite. Often, you will notice that you're either eating too much or too little. Avoiding responsibilities and procrastination is another common behavioral symptom of stress. Increased use of drugs and alcohol is also a behavioral change that will occur in most people. Nervous behaviors such as fidgeting, nail-biting and pacing can also be exhibited. When faced with stress, there are certain behavioral responses that would begin to take shape in your life.

Lack of Motivation

Stress should not be overlooked, especially with regards to unfulfilled goals and lack of motivation amongst people. Stress has shown to have a negative impact on motivation. In fact, scientists now believe that willpower is finite simply because its power can be affected by excessive levels of stress. It should be noted that sometimes the desire to succeed is closely tied to one's stress levels. Most people tend to think that motivation is a personality trait, and we tend to assume that people can't succeed because they lack motivation. In reality, motivation is more than just a personality trait. Despite the strong desire that one has to succeed, if they have a lot to deal with, their levels of motivation will be affected. When going through a lot of stress, motivation can simply fade away.

To clearly understand this, consider how a car operates. Assuming that a car uses willpower as fuel, every time the car meets a headwind, more fuel is required to propel it forward. The greater the resistance the car faces, the more willpower it uses. Now, if one is not satisfied with their work, for example due to the environment, the paycheck, or the daily tasks, all those factors all combine into a major source of discontentment, and an individual in such a situation will burn more willpower to cope.

When you keep using up your willpower every day, you will feel exhausted come nightfall. This leads to a situation where even small challenges will appear unbearable. It's imperative that you understand this clearly. Most people out there think that the people who cannot achieve their goals are lazy. You may have had the same thoughts about someone that has not accomplished their goals, or even about yourself. Yet, the reality is that stress may be responsible for sapping their motivation: stress is effectively standing between them and their vision or goals.

Change in Social Behaviors

Stress can also have a major impact on how you interact with the people around you. Normally, stress leads to social withdrawal. For instance, you might think that avoiding social gatherings is the best way of ensuring that people don't ask you questions about your career. Perhaps you feel that your career is not as good enough as compared to that of your friends. With this mentality, you could choose to disconnect.

Change in Sex Drive

Everyday stress can also have a major impact on your libido. Increased worry about deadlines at work, money, and other problems can lead to low libido. Unfortunately, this could be a major source of discontentment in your relationship. As discussed above, stress triggers the release of chemicals such as epinephrine and cortisol. These hormones should help your body deal with stress, but in excessive amounts, they will do more harm than good. Chances are that they will cause a reduction in your sex drive.

Stress and anxiety can affect your behavior, your thoughts, your feelings and your overall health. Being able to point out the common stress triggers that affect you helps to effectively manage your levels of stress and anxiety. From this chapter, you now realize that stress can cause a lot of harm in your life. You might blame the stars and luck because things are not working out for you. However, stress could be the main reason why you're suffering.

Chapter 2: General Tactics for Coping and Handling Stress

Before getting into the details about implementing effective relaxation techniques, it's important to tip you on the general tactics for coping with stress and anxiety. This chapter dives in to discuss the practical ways in which you can learn to cope with stress. Just to be clear, stress is nothing to joke with. There are millions of people out there who suffer in silence. Did you know that about 40 million adults in the United States suffer from stress and anxiety (Ducharme, 2018)? If you feel that life is weighing down on you because there's too much to handle, you're not alone. Follow the tips in this chapter to master how to deal with stress, especially in the fast-paced environment we live in today.

Practical Tips to Cope with Stress

Realize that You Cannot Control Everything

One way of coping with stress and anxiety is to admit that you have no control over everything. The only thing that you can do is change how you react towards situations that you encounter. Your relationship is not working out, maybe you're not the one to be blamed. Put your stress in perspective. Do you think it's as bad as you think? Maybe you're going through a financial quagmire because of the wrong decisions you made in the past. It has nothing to do with your personality. As such, you can choose to change how you react, for example, by choosing to accept responsibility for your mistakes and start making the right decisions from today.

Do Your Best

People often find themselves stressed because they have failed to accomplish their goals in life. When you feel that you've fallen short of your expectations, there is a likelihood that you will feel overwhelmed. Destructive thoughts will occupy your mind as you may think that you're not good enough. Cut yourself some slack! Who said that you should be perfect in everything that you do? Instead of aiming for perfection, strive for excellence. Be proud of your abilities and celebrate all the progress you make along the way. Remember, the point here is to build your confidence in positivity. Sure, things might not have turned out as you had planned, but you're proud of yourself because you did your best.

Maintain a Positive Attitude

An admirable aspect of successful people is that they understand how to leverage the power of positive thinking. These individuals stand out from the rest of us simply because they understand the power of their thoughts. The notion that you can change your world by changing your thoughts is just phenomenal. In fact, it seems too good to be true.

Maintaining a positive attitude is easy when everything is going your way. Your career is working out, your business is profitable, your relationships are fruitful, etc. All these good feelings can make you feel good about your life. On the contrary, when everything seems to be crumbling down on you, you may struggle to see anything positive about what is going on. Usually, it's at this point that your positive attitude is put to the test.

The notion of maintaining a positive attitude means that you should do your best to replace negative (destructive) thoughts with positive ones. With this positive mindset, you will always see the good in everything, whether good or bad. So, if your business is running on losses, you may consider this as an opportunity to learn something new about mitigating losses. If your marriage is on a rocky path, this could be an opportunity to renew your vows and remind each other how you feel. The idea here is that you should look for the good in everything that happens to you.

Identify Your Anxiety Triggers

It's not easy to solve a problem when you don't know the root cause of it. To effectively cope with stress, you should start by understanding your anxiety triggers. Is it your financial situation, your family, your work, or something else that is eating you up? Journaling how you feel every time you are stressed can help you identify potential anxiety triggers. This is because you will be better placed to point out existing patterns in how you react towards stress.

In the process of identifying the underlying causes of stress, try to categorize these reasons into three groups. First, classify the reasons you think you can find a solution. Secondly, group together the things that you think will get better with time. And third, put together the things you have no control over.

Once you're done with the above exercise, understand that you don't have to worry about the things in the second and third categories. For a start, some of these things will get better with time, so there is no reason for you to ruminate about them. On the other hand, some of the root causes of your stress are beyond your control. The best you can do to ensure that they don't affect you is by accepting things as they are and move on.

Limit Alcohol and Caffeine

Alcohol and caffeine are stimulants. This means that they can fuel your anxiety. High doses of caffeine and alcohol can increase your stress levels. If this continues, you may risk suffering from other mental health issues such as anxiety and depression. Drinking plenty of water can help in fighting the urge to consume coffee.

Eat Healthy

You are what you eat. Besides engaging in relaxation exercises, managing stress also requires you to eat healthy foods. Healthy foods provide the body with essential nutrients that would help in preventing negative effects of stress such as inflammation and oxidation. We also know that healthy foods contribute positively to maintaining a healthy weight.

The problem that most people face these days is that their tight schedules do not make it easy for them to prepare and eat healthy meals. It's easy for people to jump into fat-laden or sugar-rich foods as a way of treating themselves. As part of ensuring that you reduce or manage your stress levels, it is important that you develop a habit of eating healthy foods.

If you know that you might be tempted to turn to junk foods, embrace the idea of preparing your food at home. This reduces the likelihood of eating unhealthy meals. Of course, you will be more mindful of the meals you prepare. Hence, there is a good chance that you will eat healthy.

Exercise

Dieticians will often advise you that the best remedy to stress is exercising regularly. Putting physical stress on your body helps to alleviate mental stress and anxiety. There are several reasons behind this, including the fact that working out helps to lower the body's stress hormone like cortisol. Ultimately, you stand to benefit because the body will be releasing more of the feel-good chemicals (endorphins) that improve your mood. This is one of the main reasons why people feel good about themselves after exercising.

Another benefit of exercising is that it improves the quality of your sleep. After working hard at the gym or hitting the jogging trail, you will get better rest at night. Stress and anxiety can affect the quality of your sleep since your mind never stops thinking. One effective way of helping your mind to calm down is exercising. More about this will be detailed later in this guide.

Take Time Out

Sometimes the best way of coping with an overwhelming situation is to take some time out. You might push yourself to the limit hoping that things will work out fine, but in the end, you get the same results. All you need to do is to take a break. Stress can take a huge toll on you. In normal situations, people might see you as a loving and kind person. However, when you're stressed, all the positive traits that people see in you can fade away. Stress can, therefore, affect your relationships because it tends to mute your good personality traits.

It's crucial that you strike a balance between being responsible for other people and giving yourself some alone time. Realize that it's okay to take care of yourself from time to time. Self-care will go a long way in ensuring that you find yourself and cope with stress in a more reasonable manner. As such, consider taking some time to reflect and think about what you need and not what other people need from you. This is good for your mental and emotional health.

Practically, there are numerous ways of dealing with stress and anxiety. The most important thing to understand is that the way you react matters a great deal. There are situations where you might not have control over the problems you're experiencing. However, based on the ABC model you learned about in chapter 1, you have power over your thoughts. You can change what you choose to believe. Instead of believing that you cannot solve the problems at hand, realize that you have the power to reframe these problems. You can do this by viewing these problems from a positive perspective. Simply have a positive attitude towards the world around you and you will attract good things into your life.

Chapter 3: The Basics of Relaxation Techniques

You now understand the impact that stress and anxiety can have on your life. Chronic stress can put you at risk of suffering from health complications such as digestion issues, high blood pressure, anxiety, and depression, among others. Relaxation techniques are meant to help you enter into a calm state of mind. It's only when you're feeling calm that you are able to manage stress and reduce your anxiety levels. This chapter introduces you to the basic relaxation techniques that will be discussed in detail in this manual. In this section, you will understand what relaxation techniques are and the benefits that you should expect by practicing them regularly as advised.

What Are Relaxation Techniques?

Simply put, relaxation techniques refer to the strategies which are used to help in reducing levels of stress and anxiety (Star, 2012). It should be made clear that the relaxation techniques that will be discussed herein are not just meant to help you achieve a peaceful state of mind. These strategies are meant to guarantee that you manage stress and anxiety in a way that doesn't affect your health and wellbeing.

Perhaps you have been struggling with overwhelming levels of stress and anxiety and you might have been wondering whether there is a natural remedy to your condition. Relaxation techniques can help you free yourself from your mind. As previously discussed, one of the root causes of stress is your own thoughts. Accordingly, if you can master how you relax your mind, you can reduce stress and anxiety.

Your body will enter into a state of fight-or-flight when faced with stressful situations. In normal situations, this stress response is meant to help you deal with an environment where there is a potential threat. This means that some levels of stress and anxiety are good for the body. Chronic stress, on the other hand, is unhealthy. When dealing with this form of anxiety disorder, the stress response is activated frequently in the body. It causes unpleasant physical symptoms like increased heart rate, increased sweating, rapid breathing, and others.

Relaxation strategies have an opposite effect to that of the stress response. With the help of these techniques, your mind and body will be able to relax. Your heartbeat is lowered, bodily tensions reduced, and destructive thoughts decreased. Through the relaxation feeling that you will gain, you will garner an increased sense of self-worth and your problem-solving skills would be improved considerably.

Why Relaxation is So Important

Perhaps you are wondering: why is relaxation so important? Where do I get the time to relax? If someone told you that you need to relax, the first question that you would want to ask them is where do you get the time to relax? Maybe you're always on the go, doing what you can to ensure that your kids have a bright future. Indeed, the hustle and bustle of life have put us in a situation where we think that being busy is the only way to succeed. The fast-paced environment that we live in has blinded us from realizing the importance of taking some time to relax.

We often forget the importance of stepping away from the things that contribute to our stress and anxiety levels. What we fail to realize is that such relaxation bestows us with the energy we need to handle our daily stressors. It's important to reiterate the fact that not all stress is bad. Mild stress can push us into doing something that is beneficial for ourselves. However, going through high levels of stress frequently can pose detrimental effects to our mental, physical, and emotional health.

Stress overload can result in physical symptoms such as tension in the shoulders and neck, headaches, fatigue, dizziness, poor sleep patterns, etc. Since the brain will be releasing cortisol hormone more often, your mental state also stands to be affected. You will often find yourself worrying too much, overthinking things beyond proportion, having trouble making decisions and being afflicted with poor concentration. You likely feel like you've lost control of your thoughts and that your mind is controlling you. Emotionally, you will feel burdened with lots of anxiety and diminished self-esteem. This could lead to depression. Your behavior will also change since you lack control of your thoughts and emotions. People may find you aggressive or, anti-social, or you may indulge in self-destructive behavior like abusing drugs and alcohol.

Every time you put your body and mind in a state of relaxation, you increase the flow of blood around your body. This means that energy is spread through all corners of your system. The benefit gained here is that you will have a more calm and clearer mind that is able to make the right decisions at the right time. The more you make the right decisions, the more you build your life on positivity. Relaxation reduces your blood pressure by lowering your heart rate. In turn, this relieves tension in your body. With the increased blood flow throughout your system, digestion will also improve.

Normally, when your body and mind are stressed, this results in abnormal behavioral and emotional responses. You could be angered by a petty issue just because you're stressed. It's also easy to get frustrated when things don't turn out as you had expected. Relaxation reduces the likelihood of these experiences happening. With the clear state of mind that you will attain, you will be better placed to react well to stress and anxiety. You will be more aware of your thoughts. This results in a mindful way of approaching the daily challenges that seem to weigh you down.

There is a big difference between relaxing at the end of the day while staring at the TV or browsing through your social media pages and practicing relaxation strategies that will be discussed in this guide. Relaxation demands that you should change your pace of life. Activities that will help you relax include using relaxation techniques such as deep breathing, visualization, progressive muscle relaxation, physical meditation, and body scan. These relaxation strategies are helpful since they bring your mind and body in a state of true inner peace.

Prepare Your Mindset

The concept of relaxation might sound easy, but most people will still struggle when told to relax their bodies and minds. The tricky aspect of relaxation is that it requires you to refocus your mind. Of course, there are certain things that you may be worried about on a regular basis. Maybe you're stressing over work or family problems. Financial challenges that you may be experiencing could fill your mind with destructive thoughts about your future. For you to reap the health benefits of relaxation, it's crucial that you refocus your mind off these issues. You should picture yourself feeling happy and grateful for the good things that you have or you anticipate having.

You may have the impression that refocusing your mind is challenging because there is a lot going on in your life. Well, this is where our guided meditation will help you. Breathing and physical meditation techniques will help you listen to your thoughts and refocus them.

The relaxation techniques discussed in this guide are meant to help you transform your life in general. But before this happens, you have to develop a positive mindset towards what you will be doing. Think about the pain that you have been through all these years or the past few months/weeks. Maybe life has pushed you to the point where you feel like giving up. You might have been feeling like everything is a struggle. You've always been working hard and nothing seems to work out. It could also be that your personal issues have been weighing you down and this has affected all facets of your life..

As previously noted in chapter 1, stress can quickly extinguish your motivation. The mere fact that you haven't achieved your goals doesn't mean that you're lazy or unlucky. Stress and anxiety could be the root cause of all the problems that you're going through. It is for this very reason that before you start practicing the relaxation techniques in this guide you need to ensure that you know your goal.

Develop a positive mindset towards everything that you would be doing to ensure that you manage your stress and lower your anxiety levels. You should realize that the journey towards achieving a peaceful state of mind might not be easy from the get-go. Nevertheless, it is through your continued practice of these relaxation techniques that you will master how to put your body and mind in a state of tranquility.

So, expect your mind to wander from time to time. You've never done this before. As such, it's normal for your mind to think about negative things when you're trying to focus on the positive. When this happens, you should increase your awareness of your thoughts and recognize that your mind is roaming. This is what breathing and body scan techniques will teach you. It's okay to make mistakes while practicing the relaxation techniques for the first few times. Sure, you might not do it right as recommended in the manual, so aim to improve but don't beat yourself up about it. Strive to achieve a calmer state of mind each time you practice the relaxation techniques in this book. If you focus on daily improvement, rest assured that you will master how to relax your body and mind and benefit from it.

Finding Time to Relax

In line with the idea of relaxation, we cannot overlook the concept of time. Most people will jump into the idea of relaxation with the hope that they will find it easy to remember to practice relaxation techniques every day. The joy of trying out a new challenge might inspire you to start on a high note. Then life happens, and you suddenly realize that you don't have time to engage in these relaxation techniques daily as you might have wanted.

This is the same thing that happens to people when they start exercising. At the beginning, things appear interesting simply because you're doing something new. With time, the exhilaration fades away. Before you know it, you're prioritizing other mundane things over exercising. It's not until later that you again realize that exercising is important for your mind and body.

In reality, life can get busy. Usually, the demands of life can blind us from realizing that it's important to take some time off to unwind and relax. This makes it very important to find ways of fitting relaxation strategies into your tight schedule. Don't just assume that you will practice relaxation techniques in the morning and in the evening. It's vital that you reorganize your life to guarantee that you have time to practice the relaxation techniques that will be discussed in this guide. If you want to reap the benefits of these techniques in just 7 days, consistency is key.

So, how do you find time to relax?

Record How You Spend Time

The secret to finding time for your relaxation practice is to record how you use time. Start by evaluating your schedule to determine whether there are certain activities that rob you of your precious time. With the digitized environment that we live in, there are plenty of "time thieves" that you can point to. Some of these thieves include the television, the internet, and even toxic people. For instance, you may not realize that you spend more than 40 minutes every day browsing through your social media pages. Why don't you consider allocating this time to relax? After all, some of the relaxation techniques in this guide take less than 30 minutes.

Outsource Activities

Another effective way of finding some relaxation time is by outsourcing some activities. There are times where we are too busy to realize that we cannot do everything ourselves. Delegating tasks can help you gift yourself some free time to practice self-care through relaxation strategies.

Learn to Say No

It's also important to learn to say no to some of the tasks that are assigned to you. Don't take on tasks that you cannot handle. You may think that saying no is offensive, but from a positive perspective, saying no also means giving yourself some free time. You can use this time to relax your body and mind as a way of coping with stress and anxiety.

Focus on Your Breath

Despite all your efforts to find the time, you might realize that you actually don't have time at all. Well, guess what? You can practice breathing relaxation techniques in just a few minutes. You can take a few minutes in a quiet place and focus on your breath for less than 5 minutes. The good thing is that you can also do this even while in a tense environment. More about this will be discussed in detail later in this guide.

Unplug

Most individuals who are used to browsing through the internet think that this is the best way to kill time and relax. Unfortunately, the information that you feed your mind through these pages does more harm than good. Instead of picking your smartphone to browse, why don't you use this time to practice the breathing exercise that serves you best? At the end of the day, you would have lowered your stress levels and you will feel more energized and readier to tackle any challenges that pop up.

Win Your Day in the Morning

Start your day on a positive note by waking up early. The advantage of waking up early is that you get some extra hours to engage in activities that you wouldn't have found time to do later in the day. In this case, you should make a habit of meditating in the morning. This allows you to win your day in the morning. Starting your day on a good note with positive affirmations can help you achieve more in life. With this mindset, you can effectively manage stress better.

Make an Appointment - With Yourself

It's also imperative that you schedule in your "me-time." Consider your relaxation time as any other important appointment that you need to attend to. Noting down that you have an appointment with yourself will increase the likelihood of engaging in the activity. Remember, you're the one to benefit from the relaxation strategies that will be looked at. You've been suffering for too long in silence and it's time to overcome your anxiety and stress. Commit yourself to the process and you will reap the benefits in just a few days.

Now that you understand what relaxation techniques are and their relevance, let's move on to the next chapter where you start preparing yourself for the first relaxation strategy. It's important that you read chapter 3 before moving to chapter 4. You have to develop the right mindset to allow the relaxation techniques to help you. Without this, it would be difficult for you to notice any change in terms of relaxing your mind and body. When this happens you might be discouraged since the techniques discussed might not work. For that reason, mental preparation is key to ensuring that you reap the benefits of taking time to relax.

Chapter 4: The Examination Phase; Be Your Own Doctor

Usually, before a doctor can determine what you're suffering from, they will consider the symptoms that you're experiencing. Your symptoms will help them ensure that you're provided with the right medication. In the same way, managing stress and anxiety requires that you understand the symptoms that you're displaying. Symptoms of stress will vary from one person to the other. This is because people cope with stress differently. Some people might consider certain symptoms as mild. Others might find similar symptoms as overwhelming. Accordingly, it's important to understand how stress affects you from a personal perspective.

This chapter requires you to examine yourself as you strive to understand how stress affects your body and your overall well-being. This personal assessment is meant to help you become aware of your thoughts, emotions, behavior, and reactions to your immediate environment. To help you perform this self-assessment, we will define some of the signs and symptoms of stress overload.

Signs and Symptoms of Stress Overload

Cognitive Symptoms

Stress can be something that occurs to you more frequently than not. Chances are that you find yourself constantly worrying about your future or the mistakes you've made in the past. It could also be that you're not certain about what's going on in your life. Your friends and family might have pointed out to you that you always seem stressed. In reality, stress can cause numerous problems in your life, especially with regard to your cognitive abilities. The following are cognitive symptoms that will indicate that you need to manage stress before it causes more harm to your life.

Constant Worry

Do you often find yourself worrying about things that haven't happened yet? Maybe you keep thinking about "What if?" What if things go wrong in the near future? If you find yourself asking these questions, then you're stressed. Individuals who constantly worry increase their anxiety levels. In turn, this contributes to increased levels of stress. While it's okay to worry about something, excessive worry can affect your mental health. People who constantly worry will even worry when things are running smoothly.

Forgetfulness

You may also find yourself forgetting about important things in your daily routine. If this is the case, it could be an indication that you're dealing with stress overload. At work, you could find yourself forgetting about important projects that ought to have been completed. The same thing will affect your personal life as you might forget crucial family events. Forgetting things is normal. Nevertheless, in extreme cases, it can cost you your job or your relationships.

Disorganization

If you notice that people around you are complaining about your disorganized way of life, they could be pointing you to a red flag that you're stressed. When you're disorganized, you could find yourself misplacing things that are important to you. In fact, you may also mistakenly get rid of items that are essential. Your disorganized nature could also influence how you prioritize tasks. Ultimately, this will affect your productivity.

Trouble Focusing

Do you struggle to focus on a single task or activity? When you're stressed, there is a lot going on in your mind. As such, mental clutter will prevent you from concentrating. If you cannot focus on one task at a time, you will definitely struggle to finish tasks on time. Your productivity will be affected and this will lead to more stress.

Racing Thoughts

If you notice that your mind can't seem to calm down, then this is another sign of stress. Racing thoughts can affect your decision-making abilities. One minute you're thinking about doing something and the next minute your mind is thinking about a different thing. This can prevent you from taking any action because you're not sure of the right thing to do. Often, such indecisiveness leads to stress and anxiety. At the end of the day, you may choose to do nothing because you're too afraid of making mistakes. The problem is that failing to take action only contributes to more and more stress piling up. Accordingly, if you feel that your mind is constantly racing with all kinds of thoughts, this could be a sign of distress.

Poor Judgement

People who are stressed are more likely to make the wrong decisions simply because they feel overwhelmed. When there is a lot going in your life, you may want to say yes to everything just to get people out of your way. Since you will be making hasty decisions, chances are that you will make the wrong judgment calls that would affect your personal and professional life. In most cases, you will find that you keep regretting making certain decisions. This happens because you never gave things a second thought to determine whether you were making the right decision or not.

Pessimistic Outlook

Individuals who suffer from chronic stress tend to focus only on the negative. Stress can make your life miserable. Since your mind is filled with destructive thoughts, it's difficult to notice anything good in whatever happens to your life, and you will always expect the worst to happen. Your motivation will fade away since you have a pessimistic outlook towards things. Therefore, you will expect to fail in everything that you do. Of course, you cannot succeed if you keep focusing on negativity.

Psychological and Emotional Symptoms

Stress can also affect your psychological and emotional wellbeing. Some of the signs to look out for are succinctly discussed in the following lines.

Depression

Stress can also manifest to you in the form of a persistent or severe low mood. This is what the Anxiety and Depression Association of America (ADAA) defines as depression. There is a strong correlation between high levels of stress and the early stages of depression. If you feel that you're always feeling low, it is a clear sign that you're stressed.

Anxiety

Anxiety is where you are faced with overwhelming dread. You might not be sad, but you are feeling overwhelming fear about what might happen. This is where you fill your mind with "what ifs" questions. The issue here is that you dread things that you create in your mind. You might be worried thinking that you will get fired or that your spouse will leave you. These are just destructive thoughts occupying a lot of space in your mind. Constant worry can ultimately lead to stress.

Tension

Tension is also another common symptom of stress. While some tension is considered helpful, constant tension can ultimately contribute to increased levels of stress. Usually, tension can arise if you're dealing with a difficult relationship. Maybe you're always clashing with your partner. Too much competition around you can also make you tense more often. In this regard, instead of doing things normally, tension can make you feel as though there is a lot of pressure to deal with. At the end of the day, this will affect your performance.

Some reasonable level of tension is helpful. It's there to encourage you to take the necessary steps in saving a situation. If there is a strain in your relationship, tension should motivate you to take corrective measures to resolve the issue. Tension should be a short-term feeling that disappears after some time. If you find yourself feeling constantly tensed, then it shows that you need to make major changes in your life.

Insecurity

You might also feel insecure because of the varying psychological signs of stress. When you feel insecure, it may affect how you think about yourself. For instance, you might end up thinking that you add no value to the world around you. At work, you could think that you're underperforming.

Harsh self-judgment and unhelpful comparisons could make you feel inferior to the people around you. Individuals who suffer from stress will struggle appreciating what they have or what they are capable of achieving. Usually, this is what contributes to insecurity.

At times when things appear to be getting out of control, it's easy for one to believe that they are responsible. This can undermine your self-worth. It should be noted that self-worth is not necessarily defined by what you achieve. Rather, it's defined by who you are. Raising your self-esteem helps ensure that you build courage towards such psychological symptoms of stress.

Disengagement

To be honest, there are times when we all feel like we are not motivated to work. It's a normal experience to go through. After all, you cannot be motivated 24/7. However, in other cases, such a lack of motivation may spin out of control. You may constantly feel like the job you are doing is just there to help you earn something at the end of the day. This negative feeling could lead to disengagement.

There are also situations where you find yourself falling behind in the expectations that you had set for yourself. Maybe you had planned to achieve something in two or three months, but you fell short. So, you strive to do more with the hopes of catching up. Gradually, this leads to disengagement from life. You begin focusing too much on work as you spare little time to make real connections, finding less time to engage in activities that you love.

In terms of work, it gets to a point where you lose focus on what's important. You become obsessed with revenue, income, or the quantity of work you deliver. Indeed, this is what is termed as disengaging. One of the most important things that you can lose in life is purpose. You lose purpose in what you do. As you lose touch with people who would have made life meaningful to you, you find no joy in doing what you do. You end up feeling like your life is a constant vicious cycle where you're not achieving anything.

In extreme cases, you may ask yourself, "What's the point of doing all this if I am not going to be happier?" The truth is that you need to re-engage with life. This means making meaningful connections with the people around you. In a way, this will help you create your own happiness.

Isolation

Your job or other life situations may also leave you feeling isolated from time to time. This might make you feel left out. If there are problems that you may be going through, you could feel like there is no one to talk to or that no one can help you. The problem with repeated isolation is that it could make you drift away from people. Bit by bit you lose connections with important people in your life. This might go on until it gets to a point where you feel like you need to open up to someone and you have no one to turn to.

Unfortunately, the people around you might not notice that you're absent. This is because people are too busy dealing with their own problems.: they might mean no harm but you may be suffering in silence.

Psychological symptoms can affect your life in many ways. The problem with these symptoms is that they are difficult to notice. People around you might not realize that you're suffering simply because they cannot see or understand the inner workings of your mind. It's only when you open up to others that they will be able to help you.

Behavioral Symptoms

Problems are easily solved if you can identify their root cause. The same principle applies when you're dealing with stress. Your behaviors can also help you identify if you are suffering from stress. Compared to psychological and cognitive symptoms of stress, behavioral symptoms can easily be identified. The people around you might also notice your change of behavior due to stress. This doesn't mean that you should wait for people to tell you that your behavior has changed. As part of ensuring that you enjoy life, it's crucial that you heighten your awareness of likely behavioral symptoms. Some of these symptoms are described as follows.

Sleeping Difficulties

Getting a good night's sleep often requires one to relax. If you keep ruminating about the past and the future, this can leave you feeling worried and anxious. It may be challenging to shut down your brain and go to sleep. It's for this reason that people who are stressed will often toss and turn all night.

Life as we know it is quite challenging. People have a lot of pressure to deal with every day. Normally, people go the extra mile of sacrificing their sleep to ensure that they meet their goals and aspirations. Getting fewer hours of sleep might appear as the best way of keeping pace with your daily activities. Nevertheless, the importance of sleep to your optimal health should not be ignored.

Failure to get the right amount of sleep can affect your productivity the following day. You will feel tired and chances are that you might want to skip some important activities just because you need to rest. If you continue suppressing your sleep, there is no denying the fact that you will lag behind in your performance. This will contribute to increased levels of stress. You can't seem to get things done on time. Negative emotions will take a huge toll on you and stress will keep mounting.

Lack of Productivity

Timekeeping becomes a huge problem when an individual is stressed. The issue here is that you might overwhelm yourself by taking on too many tasks that you cannot handle. You could also avoid tasks since you are trying to avoid responsibility. Procrastination could also be the reason why you keep pushing tasks until the last minute. This is a common trait of people who are stressed.

It should be made clear that your poor time management skills might not explicitly imply that you're stressed. If you've been managing time well and all of a sudden you notice that you waste a lot of time, this could be an indication that something is not right. Maybe you're finding it a challenge to keep up with some tasks that you used to find easy to handle. Sometimes you may even feel like you're overloading yourself with things you cannot handle. Your lack of productivity should be well checked as it could indicate that you're dealing with stress.

Withdrawal

Stress will have a significant impact on your self-confidence and self-esteem. When you're stressed, coping with social situations becomes a major issue. Avoidance behavior will slowly creep in and you will do your best to avoid social situations to protect your fragile self-esteem.

Sometimes you may not even notice that you're withdrawing because you tend to assume that it's a common thing to do. For instance, your friends might invite you for lunch but you may choose to avoid going because you think that you cannot cope with a large group of people. You may also avoid work because you don't trust yourself to handle a particular task. Such signs of withdrawal should not be taken lightly. They are an indication that you're likely dealing with stress and anxiety.

Exhaustion

A person who is stressed will often feel like they are running from one emergency situation to another. This means that they may not find enough time to rest. If you constantly feel fatigued, it could be an indication that you're feeling overwhelmed and that you're stressed.

Addictive Behavior

Individuals who are stressed might live in denial for too long. They might not realize that they are stressed until it's too late to turn back. In situations where individuals are unaware that they are stressed, they could resort to short-term solutions to help them feel good. They may turn to drugs and alcohol looking for relief. What people may fail to realize is that such short term solutions have harmful long term consequences.

The idea of turning to drugs and alcohol as a way of dealing with stress should be the last thing on your mind.

If you drink or use drugs to escape from a situation that you don't want to handle, then you have a dependency issue. You should realize that it's better to face your problems than drowning them in alcohol or any other drugs. Your problems will not go away just because you chose to ignore them. In fact, the more you keep ignoring them, the bigger the problems get. Ultimately, you will want to drink more to free your mind from having to think about the problem. This is where you become addicted.

Unhealthy Eating Habits

Stress also drives people to seek comfort in what they eat. Most people will want to snack on unhealthy foods since they provide temporary relief to a bad feeling that one might have been going through. It's that good feeling that you get when you eat French fries that makes you want to eat more of them when you're feeling down. These foods are not nutritious, and such overindulgence can lead to health-related diseases such as high blood pressure, obesity, and heart disease among others.

People respond differently to stress. While some might overeat, others will avoid eating. Usually, this happens when individuals have negative perceptions of their self-image. It can also occur when they have negative attitudes towards food. Whatever the reasons that you might have to avoid food, devastating effects can be felt if this is left unchanged.

There is a good reason why you're always advised to eat right. Eating healthy foods provides your body with important nutrients for optimal functioning, while unhealthy foods stop you from performing at your best. Think about it this way, when you eat healthy foods, you feel good about yourself. You know that you have made the right decision and this evokes some good feelings. Eating unhealthy foods, on the other hand, makes you worry. You may be worried that you will slowly gain weight or suffer any negative effects of your bad eating habits.

This chapter has opened your eyes to the realization that you can be your own doctor. This means that you can perform a self-evaluation test before turning to the relaxation techniques that will be described in this guide. It is very important that you understand the significance of knowing the stress symptoms that you display. Arguably, by raising your awareness of these symptoms, you will be better placed to effectively manage your stress. This is something that you can do every time you notice that you're showing some of the signs that have been discussed herein.

Don't allow stress and anxiety to weigh you down while you can utilize the relaxation techniques outlined in this guide to manage your situation. You deserve to be happy and you owe it to yourself to use relaxation techniques to calm your mind and find inner peace.

Chapter 5: Breathing Techniques Guide

Take a deep breath in. Pause for a second and let it out. How do you feel after that? You may notice that there is a sudden relief that your body goes through with such deep breathing. Breathing exercises are a powerful tool to help you ease your stress and anxiety. Making these exercises part of your daily routine can make a huge difference in your ability to manage stress and lower your levels of anxiety.

In this chapter, you will garner insights on how to use breathing to increase your awareness of your inner self. You will also learn how to use these breathing exercises to release tension in your body and relax. More importantly, you will know how to reduce or relieve symptoms of stress.

Introduction to Breathing

Every day there are certain activities on our to-do list that we consider normal. We tend to think about some of these activities frequently, for example, eating and drinking. In fact, if you're thirsty, you might be thinking about finding a glass of water. The same case applies if you're hungry. You may be thinking about your next meal.

Remarkably, there are certain things that we do every single day, yet we don't think about them at all. When was the last time you thought about how you're breathing? Maybe this is something that you never think about unless you have a bad cold or you engage in long-distance running. Often, people take breathing for granted. The interesting thing about life is that it goes on even when you're not conscious about it.

Breathing is integral for your survival. Your life depends on it. With each breath you take, you breathe in life: you take oxygen into the body and release carbon dioxide as the waste product.

Your lungs are the organs responsible for your breathing. The lungs are part of the respiratory system. You may not see your lungs, but you can easily feel them at work each time you breathe in and out.

Place your hands on your chest. Take a deep breath in and out. As you breathe in, your chest expands. As you breathe out, your chest returns to its usual size. The expanding and contracting of your chest is because of your lungs in action.

You know how to breathe, but chances are that you might not be making maximum use of your lungs. Unfortunately, this leaves you wasting away every breath of extra energy that you would have taken advantage of. You're not alone. Most people are never conscious of their breathing. In the modern day, poor breathing habits are quite common. As previously noted, it is very likely that you've never thought about the intimate relationship that exists between your breathing, your mind, and your body.

It is worth pointing out that by being conscious of your breathing, you have the power to transform and strengthen both your mind and your body. Human beings are capable of transforming themselves to a degree that beats scientific understanding. Unfortunately, modern life has pushed people to extremes and they take their breathing for granted. People are rushing day and night to earn a living and this has disconnected us from our bodies. The negative effect experienced here is that we obliviate the peaceful and deep breathing gift we were bestowed with at birth.

Fortunately, it's never too late to start listening to your body. The breathing exercises discussed herein should help you reconnect with your body and mind, and reap the benefits of the calmness you gain.

Effectiveness of Breathing in Relieving Symptoms of Stress and Anxiety

Breathing exercises are a great tool to get more in touch with your body, mind and spirit. Conscious breathing can help in bringing your mind to the present moment. Equally, such breathing can help bring your attention to the energy of your emotions. When negative emotions seem to weigh you down, conscious breathing can increase your awareness of these emotions and how they are affecting you.

Every time you are stressed, the negative energy from your emotions can take a huge toll on you. It affects how you feel, react, and how you make decisions. With the help of deep conscious breathing, you can shift your attention from the negative energy in your body. This helps in releasing the weight of these emotions which can be quite debilitating. There are other benefits to conscious breathing, including the fact that it helps increase oxygen flow and alertness. Your body can also detoxify more readily when you practice breathing repeatedly during the day. Although breathing is considered as the most natural thing to do, it's also a skill that you improve with constant practice.

Mastering the Art of Breathing

There is nothing new about breathing exercises. The only thing that you will be doing here is breathing consciously while listening to your body and mind. The benefits of breathing can be experienced immediately, or it might also take some time for you to notice a change in how you feel or how you think. With constant practice, you start reaping the benefits of conscious breathing. The goal of this guide is to ensure that you reap the benefits of breathing in 7 days or less: it's very important that you develop a daily breathing program that serves you best.

Instructions

This section is divided into three categories to ensure that you find it easy to master the art of breathing. The first thing that we will discuss is the preparation. How do you prepare yourself to breathe? What steps should you take to ensure that you realize the benefits of such breathing? Most importantly, how do you prepare yourself mentally for the process?

Next, we will look into the breathing basics. Here we will take a look at the two types of breath; chest breathing and diaphragmatic breathing. The last section will focus on breathing exercises to increase your awareness and release tension from your body.

Preparation Phase

Conscious breathing demands that you choose an appropriate time and place where you will not be disturbed. Since you're in the learning stages, it is crucial that you practice breathing in a quiet place. You should also perform these breathing exercises at the same time daily. This will make it easier for you to develop a habit that you can stick to. After mastering the art, you can breathe anywhere, especially if you find yourself in a tense situation.

As you prepare to practice breathing every day, it's important to use your nose and not your mouth. Therefore, if your nasal passages are blocked, you should find a way of clearing them. In instances where you cannot clear them, use your mouth.

Choose a relaxed position that is best for you. Depending on your purpose for breathing, you can settle in different positions. For instance, if your aim is general relaxation, breathe while seated. If you intend to soothe yourself to sleep, the best position would be lying down.

Good posture is key to ensuring that you relax your body and mind. Don't just assume any seated position. Strive for a comfortable position where your spine is well supported and your arms and legs are stretched out.

As a beginner, consider practicing breathing while lying down. This is because it's easier for you to relax your body and mind while in this position. Gradually, you can try breathing while seated. But give yourself enough time for you to master how to calm your body and mind while in this position.

There are two positions that you can assume while lying down. You can either lie down with your knees bent or with your legs stretched out and slightly apart. Nevertheless, the best position is with your knees slightly bent, because it offers you a relaxed body posture, making it easy to calm your mind while you focus on breathing.

It's important that you choose a relaxed position that suits you. Before beginning the exercise, take a few moments to scan through your body to determine whether you've assumed the right posture. While doing this, relieve tension from your body as you shift for the best position. The point is to make yourself as comfortable as possible.

Breathing Basics

How Do You Breathe?

1. First, it's important to evaluate how you currently breathe. To do this, start by closing your eyes, then put your left arm on your abdomen near the waistline. Put your right arm on your chest, at the center.
2. Pay attention to how you breathe without changing anything. The point here is to notice how air is moving in and out of your body through your nose (or through your mouth.)
3. Raise your awareness of how air is filling your lungs when you breathe in. Again, observe how air is moving out of your lungs as you breathe out.
4. As you breathe in and out, notice the movement of your hands. Which hand moves up and which one moves down?

If the hand placed on your abdomen (left arm) rises the most compared to the one on the right, then you're breathing diaphragmatically. Conversely, if the hand on your chest moves more, then you're chest breathing.

Diaphragmatic Breathing

The diaphragm refers to a large, dome-shaped muscle that is situated at the base of the lungs. Using the diaphragm correctly to breathe helps you benefit from the breathing exercises (Diaphragmatic breathing exercises & techniques, n.d.). With diaphragmatic breathing, the abdominal muscles are used to provide more power to the diaphragm muscle so that it can efficiently empty your lungs.

So, what is diaphragmatic breathing? Basically, this refers to a type of breathing intended to ensure that you use the diaphragm correctly while breathing. This results in benefits such as:

- Strengthening of the diaphragm
- Decreased oxygen demand
- Less effort and energy required to breathe
- Slowing your breathing rate

Mastering The Technique

1. Assume a lying position either in your bed or on a flat surface.
2. Use a pillow to support your head and your knees so that you take on a lying position with your knees bent.
3. Place your left hand on your chest and the right hand just below the rib cage. This position will allow you to notice how the diaphragm moves while you breathe in and out.
4. Now, take a deep breath in slowly through your nose. As you breathe in, notice how the

hand on your abdomen rises. Ensure that you don't move the hand on your chest.
5. Exhale through your nose. You can also breathe out through your pursed lips. This allows you to slow down the rate of your breathing.
6. Once you know how to use this technique, you can slow down the rate of your breathing. This can be done through your conscious effort in knowing that you're paying attention to your breath. You don't have to frown while performing this breathing exercise. Relax. Smile. Notice the body movements as you breathe in and out. Listen to your body. As you breathe out through your pursed lips, pay attention to the sound and feel of warm air as it leaves through your lips.
7. Feelings, sensations, and all kinds of thoughts might flow into your mind and this could distract you. Don't resist. Notice the presence of these thoughts and emotions and gently bring back your focus on your breathing.
8. Breathe diaphragmatically for about 5-10 minutes.
9. At the end of this exercise, pause for a moment to reflect on how you feel.

It's highly recommended that you scan through your body at the start and at the end of the exercise. This gives you the opportunity to compare how you felt before and how you feel after the exercise.

As a novice breather, it's recommended that you perform the diaphragmatic breathing while lying down. Once you've practiced enough, you can practice breathing while sitting on a chair.

Diaphragmatic Breathing on a Chair

1. Find a comfortable chair to sit on. Your knees should be bent with your back, shoulders, and neck relaxed.
2. Place your hands on your chest and on your rib cage just as you did in the above exercises.
3. Take a deep breath in slowly through your nose. While doing this, notice how your hands are moving.
4. Exhale through your nose or through your pursed lips.
5. Remember to focus on your breathing as you strive to notice your thoughts, emotions and sensations that come to you. The goal is to bring your mind to focus on your breathing regardless of what you may be feeling or thinking.

Note: At first, diaphragmatic breathing might not be easy for you. In fact, you may get tired during your first few attempts. However, it's very important that you continue practicing as it gets better with time.

So, how often should you practice this type of breathing? Start by practicing this breathing exercise for about 5-10 minutes. This can be done 3-4 times daily. With time, increase the amount of time to about 20 minutes. Once you're good at it, you can place a book on your abdomen while your hands lie stretched on either side.

Breathing for Increased Awareness and Tension Release

Mindful Breathing for Increased Awareness

Mindfulness breathing is another breathing exercise that you can utilize to increase your awareness and bring your mind to the present moment. Basically, mindfulness breathing is about focusing on your breathing. This exercise can be done standing or lying down. The point is to find a comfortable position where you will easily concentrate without getting distracted. Your eyes can be open or closed when performing this exercise. However, to ensure that you don't struggle to focus, closing your eyes is highly recommended.

With regards to time, it helps a lot to schedule your mindful breathing exercise. When you set some time aside to practice this exercise, it means that you will be doing it consciously, but this should not stop you from practicing it when you're feeling anxious or stressed during the day.

When faced with a stressful situation, make a deliberate effort to take an exaggerated breath. Inhale through your nose and pause for about 2 seconds. Exhale through your mouth while allowing all the air that you had inhaled to leave via your pursed lips. While you're inhaling and exhaling, notice any body changes without trying to change anything. For instance, pay attention to the rising and falling of your chest or the feeling of your nostrils as air moves in and out. Your mind might wander while you're doing this. It's okay. Don't resist it. Rather, notice this happening and gently shift your focus back to your breath.

To help you find it easy to practice mindfulness breathing, below are steps that you should follow.

1. Find a quiet place where you can practice mindfulness breathing without interruptions. Make yourself comfortable by either sitting on the floor or on a chair. If you choose to

sit down, ensure that your back is upright. Allow your arms to rest anywhere as long as you're comfortable.
2. Listen and connect with your body. Scan through your body while noticing your shape as you move from head to toe. Relax any points where you feel there is tension. Become curious about your body. Feel the sensations and the connection with the environment around you. Just breathe.
3. Now, listen to your breath. Just feel the natural flow of how you're breathing in and out. Don't change anything about how you're breathing. Just notice how beautiful it is to take in air and then let it out of your system. Pay attention to the places where you can feel your breath: your chest, your abdomen, your nostrils. Take one breath at a time as you try to connect with each breath.
4. In the process of listening to your body with all the silence around you, your mind might wander. There is a lot on your mind and you cannot blame yourself if your mind is wandering, thinking about things not in the present moment. It's normal for this to happen. Even people who have meditated for years often find their minds wandering.

So, don't be anxious because you cannot stop thinking about other things. Notice that your mind is wandering by whispering "wandering" or "thinking" inside your head. This raises your awareness of what is happening around you both physically and mentally. Gently shift your focus back to the breathing.
5. Maintain your focus for about 5-10 minutes. Ensure that you're noticing your breath. If your mind wanders again, bring it back to the point of focus without resisting any thoughts or sensations coming in.
6. Take a deep breath in as you conclude your exercise. Take a few moments to notice how you're feeling. Scan your body to feel the positive changes that you have experienced. Continue relaxing for a few minutes while you allow your body to relax even more. Now appreciate yourself for finding time to practice this breathing exercise.

Other Breathing Techniques to Try

Besides the common breathing techniques that have been described above, there are other techniques that you can use to reduce stress or anxiety. Some of these exercises are engaging and you may find that you find it easy to practice them every day.

Lion's Breath

This is a dynamic breathing exercise that will help relieve tensions in your face and chest. Yoga enthusiasts often term this exercise as simhasana or simply, Lion's Pose (Cronkleton, 2019).

How to do it:
1. Find a comfortable and quiet place to sit. You can cross your legs or sit on your heels.
2. Spread your legs and press your palms against your knees. Spread your fingers wide while assuming this position.
3. Take a deep breath in through your nose while you open your eyes wide.
4. As you inhale, open your mouth wide. Allow your tongue to stick out and drop it to your chin.
5. Exhale through your mouth. As you do this, make a "ha" sound. This should be a long sound as though you were imitating a lion.
6. Repeat this exercise two or three times.

When should you practice the lion's breath? This breathing exercise is best suited for times when you're looking for energy to do something. Maybe you woke up feeling moody or tired. This breathing exercise can be a great way of achieving focus and avoiding procrastination.

4-7-8 Breathing

4-7-8 breathing is also termed as "relaxing breath." Just as the name suggests, this is a simple breathing technique that involves inhaling for 4 seconds, holding your breath for 7 seconds, and breathing out for 8 seconds.

One of the main advantages of this technique is that it helps to lower your anxiety levels. Similarly, this exercise can be performed when one is looking to catch some sleep after a long tiresome day. It might sound crazy but proponents argue that this breathing exercise can make you sleep in 1 minute (Fletcher, 2019).

There are several benefits that you can gain by practicing 4-7-8 breathing including, reducing anxiety, managing cravings, getting some sleep and controlling anger responses.

How to do it:

Before you start this exercise, find a comfortable position to take. Place the tip of your tongue on the roof of your mouth right behind your front teeth. After that, focus on the following pattern:

1. Start by emptying your lungs by breathing out.
2. Now breathe in slowly through your nose for 4 seconds.
3. Hold your breath for 7 seconds. Count this to 7.
4. After that, purse your lips and exhale stoutly through your mouth. Make a "whoosh" sound while you're at it for 8 seconds.
5. Repeat the process 4 times.

So, how often should you use this breathing technique? To start noticing the benefits in days, consider practicing this technique at least twice daily. After this exercise, you may feel lightheaded, especially if you're doing it for the very first time. As such, it's strongly recommended that you perform this exercise while lying or sitting down. This will prevent falls or dizziness.

The more you practice the 4-7-8 breathing technique, the sooner you will reap its benefits. You should remember to maintain the correct ratio as advised in the steps herein.

Breath Counting

Another common breathing technique is breath counting. It is an effective breathing exercise that can help you manage stress.

1. Sit comfortably on the floor or on a chair. Keep your head up and your back straight. Ensure that you're not assuming a stiff position. It's also important that you wear something comfortable. No tight belt, shoes, bras.
2. Close your eyes and perform a body scan. Notice any tensions around your body. Scan from head to toe and let go of any tension that leaves you feeling stiff.
3. Relax and breathe. Using your diaphragm, take a deep breath in slowly through your nose. To ensure that you don't take in quick breaths, imagine having a small balloon under your belly button. Now, picture yourself inflating this balloon slowly with every breath you take.
4. With your breathing as your point of focus, for every breath you take in, count it as "one." Breathe out slowly. When you breathe in for the second time, count this as "two." Continue doing this to the count of five.

To prevent your mind from wandering, counting to five is recommended. If you continue counting past that, it is likely that you may think of other things, so it's good to keep it short for the best results.

Breathing exercises can help in gaining a calming effect since your heart rate will naturally slow down, helping you gain an opposite effect to the fight or flight response. When dealing with stress and anxiety, your breath can be a great tool to help you relax.

You may be wondering when is the best time for you to practice these breathing exercises? Breathing techniques can be performed at any time of the day. One breathing exercise can take less than five minutes. This means that you can practice breathing anytime you feel anxious or stressed. These exercises will help you relax. Instead of reacting to a situation, you will respond to it in the best way possible.

It's however recommended that you practice breathing exercises in the morning. Early morning is a special time of the day. If you live in a quiet neighborhood, you might notice the birds chirping welcoming the new day. Indeed, a new day is worth rejoicing. During this time, your mind is also booting up preparing itself for your daily routine. Starting your day on a high note has a profound impact on how you will approach your day. You will be energized since you started your day on a positive note. With your mind and body relaxed, you will approach everything from a more positive perspective. In the long run, this mentality will transform your life as you will value the importance of winning your day in the morning. Overall, don't forget to breathe when faced with a stressful situation or when your anxiety levels upsurge.

Chapter 6: Body Scan Techniques Guide

Stress and anxiety can leave you feeling tense with a lot of discomfort in your body. Sadly, our everyday stressors can be so overwhelming that you ignore the physical discomfort you may be experiencing. You're feeling pain on your shoulders or you're frequently experiencing headaches but you consider them to be normal after a tedious day. It's important to realize that the physical discomfort you're experiencing could be tied to your emotional state. Body scan meditation is a great way to relieve your body and mind of stress and anxiety. This practice doesn't just help you relax, but it aims to increase your awareness of your body from head to toe. Through your increased awareness, you can release tension from your body.

What is Body Scan Meditation?

Body scan practice is a type of meditation exercise that scans your body from head to toe. This technique is regarded as the most effective way to start mindfulness meditation. By scanning through your body from head to toe, you raise your awareness of every body part, relaxing areas of tension. During this meditation practice, your mind is brought to the present moment as you're more mindful of your body. Combining this benefit to the relaxation advantage that you gain makes this technique a powerful stress and anxiety reliever.

The goal of a body scan is to help you connect more with your body and reconnect with its physical aspect. You will be more aware of the sensations that you're feeling. Training your mind to stay in the present will be helpful in all facets of your life. You will be more accepting, you will learn to express gratitude for the things that happen in your life; overall, you will live mindfully and this will lead you to live a happy and fulfilling life.

Mastering the Practice of Body Scan

3-Minute Body Scan Meditation

To ensure that you find it easy to focus on your body scan meditation, we'll start with a short body scan practice. This scan can be performed while sitting, lying down or in any other posture, as long as you're comfortable.

1. Sit or lie down comfortably. Pay attention to your body as you start this scan.
2. Close your eyes if you find it difficult to focus.
3. Feel the weight of your body pressing on the floor or on the chair.
4. Take a long deep breath through your nose and exhale through your mouth.
5. Focus on how your body feels. Begin at the top of your head.
6. Continue scanning down your body as you notice any areas that are tense, stiff and uncomfortable.
7. Don't try to change anything. The point is to connect with your body and notice how every part feels.
8. Scan down your body, one section at a time until you reach your toes.
9. Notice the presence of your body and take a deep breath.
10. Breathe out through your pursed lips as you open your eyes.

This three-minute body scan can help bring you back to the present, especially when you feel that there is a lot going on in your mind. Don't allow yourself to ruminate as you can take advantage of this technique.

You can manage stress and anxiety effectively if you develop a habit of being present.

10-Minute Body Scan Meditation

This body scan practice should take you about 10 minutes. Before you start this exercise, ensure that you have enough time to relax. Choose a comfortable and quiet place to perform this body scan.

1. Make yourself comfortable.
2. Close your eyes.
3. Bring awareness to your body by taking a deep breath in through your nose. Breathe out gently. Notice the position of your body in your space. Pay attention to how your body touches the floor or the seat you're using. Take a few minutes to ensure that you connect deeply with your body.
4. When you're ready, take another deep breath. Notice how warm air is rushing through your nose into your lungs.
5. Gently shift your focus to your body. Start from the top of your head as you move from one section to another. One at a time. You could also start from your toes and move up towards your upper body. Pay attention to any sensations you may be feeling and let

go. Proceed with the feet slowly and move up to your ankles, calves, etc. Continue focusing on the individual parts of your body without trying to change anything. You only need to become aware of how you feel and how your body feels.

6. Sensations in your body might vary from one end to the other. You may feel pressure in other parts, whereas you might feel cramps, cold, tightness, or a tingling sensation in others. You may fail to feel these sensations and that you could feel that your body is just feeling neutral. Accept it. It's okay if this is what you're feeling. Go with the feeling that you're experiencing and continue scanning your body.

7. Strive to be curious about what's going on in your body. Make a deliberate effort to notice how each body part feels before moving to the next.

8. You may lose focus as you continue scanning your body. Observe how this is happening but don't make any judgments. Don't be frustrated that you cannot fully focus. It's normal for your mind to wander. Shift your focus back to your object of focus, your body. You can also bring your mind back to focus by paying attention to your

breath. Try counting your breath as this will stop your mind from wandering.

9. When you feel that you've performed a full-body scan, open your eyes mindfully.
10. Don't be quick to get up and leave the room. Be mindful of how you're feeling and your surroundings. Notice how the room looks, look at the furniture, the walls, and anything around you. View these things as though you were noticing them for the first time. You're now relaxed. You're at peace with yourself. Now extend these good feelings to how you approach your day.

This 10-minute body scan can be done at any time of the day. However, it's highly recommended that you schedule in time for this exercise. Consider it a crucial meeting that you must have with yourself. You should realize that your day can get so packed that you might fail to remember to perform a body scan. In some cases, you might rush to do this practice while your mind is busy thinking of how you will resume working. Accordingly, it's very important to find an appropriate time to do a meditation body scan.

Powerful 20-Minute Body Scan Meditation

Start this exercise by making yourself comfortable. You can choose to lie on the floor or sit in a chair: make sure you feel comfortable so that you can achieve the focus that is required for this body scan meditation.

Find an environment that will not allow your mind to wander. It's crucial that you perform this body scan at a time when there is little or no interruption from your family members. Turn off any electronic devices that might distract you. Consider this time as your "me-time." A time for focusing on yourself. An opportunity to reconnect with your mind, body and soul, a special time for self-care: you shouldn't take it for granted.

It's important not to try and force things around. Don't push yourself to relax. Doing this will only create tension. The best way to relax is to accept everything that is happening around you. Become aware of each passing moment. Let go of wanting to fix things. We all have a tendency to try to change things that are happening around us. Avoid this by making sure that you allow things to be just as they are.

Follow these instructions while you take time to notice any activity of the mind and body. Treat yourself with kindness. Don't be too critical of your thoughts and let go of judgment. Just become aware and accept things as they are.

Keep in mind that there is no perfect way to feel while you're performing this body scan. There is nothing wrong with how you're feeling. It's okay to feel how you're feeling. So, there is no need to try and change it for you to feel right. Understand the importance of acceptance. Allow yourself to feel how you're feeling and realize that it's totally okay.

Now, gently close your eyes if you feel comfortable meditating with your eyes shut. Move on to sense the position of your body. Consider the chair or the mat that is supporting it off the ground.

Slowly bring your attention to your breath. Become aware of how you're breathing without trying to change anything. Just listen to your body breathe in and out. Notice how your body is moving as you inhale and exhale. As you inhale, notice how your chest is rising. And as you exhale, notice your chest falling. Follow the rhythm of your breath as you cherish how good it feels to breathe naturally and be alive.

With every breath that you take, your lungs are filled with warm air. As you breathe out, allow your body to rest even more. Your mind might become distracted. Notice when this is happening and bring your attention back to the point of focus; your breathing.

Now exhale deeply as you gently shift your focus to your body. Move down to your left foot and focus on the big toe. Pay attention to any sensations that you might be feeling here. Are you feeling cold or warm? Feel the touch of the socks or the stockings on your feet. Maybe you feel nothing. Just be there and notice what's going on. Move your attention from the big toe to the other toes of your left foot. Become mindful of the toenails and the skin. How do you feel between your toes?

Now shift your attention to the heel of your left foot. Notice the contact that it has with the mat or the floor. Gradually shift your focus to the top of the foot. Feel the change of skin and the surrounding temperature. Ensure that you notice all the sensations here, including the bones. Take a deep breath in. Just imagine yourself breathing through your left foot. Breathe in and out as if you could use your foot to breathe. As you breathe in, the fresh air will bring a sense of freshness in you. And as you breathe out, you release any tightness or tension on this part of the body. Just let go.

Moving up, bring your focus to your ankle. Become aware of the tendons, the bones and the skin. How does it feel? Take a deep breath of freshness into this part and breathe out to release any tension you might be feeling. Remember, you might not be feeling anything. It's okay to not feel anything. Understand this and move on to the next part of your body.

Bring your focus to your left leg just above your ankle. Feel its contact with the floor or the mat that is holding you above ground. Become aware of the shin bone, the calf muscle, and the skin around them. Pay attention to any sensations here. Take a deep breath in and out.

Explore the knee area. Focus on your left knee joint. Examine how you are feeling at the kneecap, the hinge, the cartilage, then move to the underside area. Are there any sensations here? Bring your attention to these sensations. Breathe in some freshness to this area then breathe out to release tension. Make sure that you're not judging any feelings that you may be experiencing. Be present with the feeling, release tension, and move on.

Move up to your left thigh. Feel the muscle of the leg here and the skin. You may focus more and feel how blood is circulating around this area. There could be some slight heaviness as the thighs carry a large muscle. Become aware of the thigh bone and notice how it sits in its socket.

Take a deep breath in as you allow some sense of freshness to fill your left leg from the bottom to the thigh area. Breathe out any form of tension that may be left out. Release any tiredness that you may be feeling. Relax.

Now bring your attention back to the thigh bone and make a smooth transition to the right hip. Move all the way to your right foot and start scanning your body from the big toe of this foot. How do you feel here? Be present here and do nothing to change how you're feeling.

Slowly shift your focus to the other toes. Notice how you're feeling around the toenails and the skin. How do you feel in between your toes? Become conscious of any sensations you may be experiencing while you make a deliberate effort to shift your attention to the ball of this foot.

Move to the arch of your right foot, then the heel. Pause for a moment here to notice how the skin of the heel is different. Afterward, move to the top part of the right foot. Feel the difference when focusing on the bones in this area. Now widen your focus to include the entire right foot. Take a deep breath of fresh air and breathe out tension or any form of tightness.

Bring your focus to your right ankle. Become aware of the skin, the bones, the tendons. Gradually move up to the right leg as you feel the pumping of blood around this area. Become aware of the skin, the calf muscle, the shin bone. Slowly draw your attention to the right knee. Examine this area for a few seconds connecting with any sensations that might be here.

As you continue feeling the pulsation of blood circulation in your system, slowly move with the flow to your right thigh. Explore the feeling of the muscle and of the thigh bone. Breathe in some freshness into this area of your body. Breathe out to release toxins and congestion. Relax.

Now bring your focus to the middle area of your body, the pelvic bowl. Pay attention to your hip bones. Become aware of the organs located around this part of the body. The bladder, the reproductive organs, and the intestines. Notice how your buttocks are providing you with the support off the ground. How are you feeling around this area? Maybe you're feeling heavy or light, or perhaps you're feeling some tightness.

Move your attention up from the lower back to the spine. Pay attention to every inch of your spine as you notice how each vertebra feels. Become aware of your back muscles, your skin, and any sensations around this area. Allow your back muscles to relax with every breath you take in.

Gently bring your focus to the middle area of your back where your kidneys sit. Pay attention to the rib cage area. Become mindful of the expansion and contraction of the rib cage as you breathe in and out.

Notice where the rib cage connects with the spine, at the back of your lungs, the back of your heart or near the shoulder blades. While doing this, move further up to the area where the spine connects with the skull.

Take a deep breath in to expand your entire back area. Allow freshness to fill this area and let go of any tension. Breathe out and allow your back to rest more into the floor or the chair that you're seated on.

Bring your attention to your chest. Continue feeling the expanding and contracting of the rib cage as you inhale and exhale. Focus on how the rib cage is also moving from the sides under your armpits. Become aware of how the heart is cushioned between the lungs. As you do this, notice how the lungs and the heart are working together to help you breathe in oxygen and breathe out carbon dioxide.

Now slowly draw your awareness to your chest muscles and the breasts. Notice how the skin feels here. Take a deep breath in, bringing in rejuvenated energy within you. Fill your lungs with new energy and breathe out releasing any tightness inside you. What are some of the emotions that you feel around this area? You may or may not feel anything. Don't push yourself to change anything if you're not feeling anything. Similarly, if there are emotions that come and go, just notice them and move on. Stay aware, and not judgmental.

Move on to your arms. Start by focusing on your fingertips. Become aware of the sensation at the top of your fingertips. Perhaps you feel some dryness or moisture? How about the skin, the fingernails, the knuckles, the joints, the palms? How do you feel around this area? Breathe in some freshness to this area of your body and breathe out releasing any tightness or tension you may be feeling.

Continue with the scan raising your awareness to your upper arm, your shoulders, your throat, the back of the head, and your cheeks. It's important that you pay attention to all sensations that you may be feeling around these areas. While scanning through these areas, ensure that you maintain your neutral mindset. For every deep breath you take, consider this as your way of breathing in fresh energy into the part of your body that you're focusing on. When you breathe out, you release tension and toxins from your body.

As you approach the end of this 20-minute body scan, let go of any control that you may have. Allow yourself to be still, inhaling and exhaling freely as you notice your surroundings. Your acceptance to how things are is a form of healing that is gained through body scan meditation. As such, it's important to accept your world as it is without trying to change it.

Take a third-eye perspective and see yourself as a complete being, worthy of living the best life you can. See the fullness of your ability to live and love those who are around you. Realize that you're now fully awake and relaxed. Don't be in a rush to get up and leave the room. Take a few moments to bring your attention to your body. Notice the good feeling that flows in you at this point. Stretch gently. When you're ready, congratulate yourself for taking the time to focus on yourself. Resume your activities building on the good feeling that you gained through this relaxation technique.

Chapter 7: Progressive Relaxation Techniques Guide

Progressive muscle relaxation (PMR) is an effective relaxation technique that is often used to manage stress and anxiety. It can also help in relieving insomnia as well as symptoms of chronic pain. The basic idea behind this form of relaxation is that it involves tightening or tensing of muscles, one area at a time followed by relaxation of these muscles to release tension. When faced with stress and anxiety, it's common to feel that your muscles are tensed almost throughout the day. Practicing PMR will help you notice that there is a huge difference between tensed and relaxed muscles. Some medical experts use PMR alongside cognitive behavioral therapy techniques. However, this doesn't mean that using PMR alone is not effective. Once you master this relaxation technique, you will have a greater sense of control over how your body responds to stress and anxiety.

Preparing for Relaxation

Preparing for any relaxation technique demands that you should set aside some time to complete the exercise without any distractions. This applies when you're about to practice progressive muscle relaxation. The exercise will take about 15 minutes. Ensure that you find a quiet and peaceful place to practice PMR.

During the first few days, it's vital that you practice this technique at least twice a day. This guarantees that you master the relaxation technique as soon as possible. Remember, the faster you get the hang of it, the better. You will effectively manage your anxiety and stress. Ideally, you will approach each day full of energy and optimism. This is something that people who are anxious or stressed find impossible to accomplish.

There are a few concerns that you should bear in mind while practicing PMR. Do you suffer from any physical injuries? If you have a history of physical injuries that might lead to muscle pain or cramps, then it's crucial that you talk to your doctor about the exercises that you would be performing.

It's also vital that you select ideal surroundings to practice this technique. Minimize or prevent any distractions to your five senses. Start by turning off the TV, radio, and any electrical appliances that might distract you. Adjust your lighting to soft if possible as this will provide you with a suitable environment to concentrate.

Comfort is key to successful progressive muscle relaxation. Find a chair that makes you comfortable. Your back should be upright and your head should be well supported. Wear loose clothing to avoid any discomfort. If possible, consider taking off your shoes.

You must practice PMR while your mind and body are calm and fresh. Your ability to focus might be affected after eating a heavy meal. Accordingly, it's recommended not to practice after a big meal. The same case applies to intoxicants, like alcohol. You should realize that you cannot accurately focus with an intoxicated mind. So, make sure you do it with a fresh mind.

Instructions

Muscle tension is often associated with anxiety, stress, and panic attacks. This is the natural way in which our bodies respond to potentially dangerous situations. Some of these situations might not be life-threatening, but our bodies generally react in the same way. This is what we talked about at the beginning of this manual. It's the fight-or-flight response.

Unfortunately, a good number of people are not aware of the muscle groups which are tensed in their bodies. PMR can help you focus on different muscle groups and relax the areas where you feel tense. Just as the name suggests, progressive muscle relaxation involves a step-by-step analysis of muscle groups. So, the key issue is to move from one specific muscle group at a time. First, you feel the tension in that muscle, and then you release the tension. This is done from head to toe scanning throughout your body. With the PMR technique, you will learn to recognize specific muscle groups and to differentiate between tensed sensations and feelings of deep relaxation.

You can practice PMR while sitting on a chair or lying down. Particular muscle groups are tensed for 5-7 seconds, released and then relaxed for 20-30 seconds. The length of time can vary; you don't have to adhere to the time mentioned here strictly. It's, however, strongly recommended that you stick to the indicated time when you're practicing PMR during the first few days. This practice should be repeated at least twice daily. Of course, some muscles are harder to relax. When this happens, focus on that particular muscle tensing and releasing it for about five times.

You might be distracted during the first few attempts. Once you memorize the steps that should be followed, you can easily close your eyes and focus on one muscle group at a time.

To help you understand the practice better, the progressive muscle relaxation instructions are divided into two parts. The first section features the basic procedure. You can memorize this section and recall it while you're practicing PMR. This makes it easy for you to familiarize yourself with the different muscle groups in your body. Take frequent pauses where necessary.

The second section is shorter than the first as it focuses on tensing and relaxing several muscle groups at a time. This means that you will spend less time doing the relaxation practice.

Levels of Tensing

There are three levels of tensing you can incorporate in your PMR practice. Once you're conversant with the forms of tensing, you can settle for one that serves you best.

Active Tensing

Essentially, this level of tensing involves the simple process of actively relaxing a specific muscle group at a time. You should tense these muscle groups as tightly as you can without harming yourself. While doing this, pay attention to the resulting sensations after tensing your muscles, then relax that part of the muscle and examine how you feel. During the tension phase, it's recommended that you breathe diaphragmatically.

Tensing your muscle groups as tightly as you can help in raising your awareness about areas of your body where you often carry chronic tension. People with no history of injuries should use this form of tensing. Picture yourself carrying a heavy box for an extended period. How do you feel when you drop this box? You will feel good and relaxed, right? This is how active tensing makes you feel.

Threshold Tensing

Threshold tensing is similar to active tensing but different in the sense that you should only tense your muscles slightly. This form of tensing is ideal for areas that are very tense or injured. It's effective once you get the idea of how the basic form of active tensing works. If you have a history of injuries or chronic pain, threshold tensing comes highly recommended.

Passive Tensing

Passive tensing is where you simply notice tension in specific muscle groups. Instead of tensing your muscle groups as advised in active or threshold tensing, here you only notice areas of your body that are tensed. This type of tensing is best used when you're not feeling any tension in your body. However, all these forms of tensing are useful in helping you achieve a deepened state of relaxation.

Basic Procedure

Find a comfortable position to assume. You can either sit or lie down as long as you're comfortable. Choose a quiet room where you will not be interrupted.

Make a deliberate effort to focus on your body. Your mind might start to wonder. Notice this happening but gently bring your mind back to your object of focus, the muscles you're tensing.

Breathe in diaphragmatically through your abdomen. Pause and hold your breath for 5 seconds. Now breathe out slowly through your pursed lips. While you're breathing in and out, notice the movement of your chest and your stomach. This helps your mind to stay focused and in the present moment.

As you breathe out, imagine tension being released out of your body. For every breath you take, you breathe in some fresh air that brings in relaxation to tense muscles in your body. Breathe in... and out. Feel your body already relaxing.

From this moment onwards, remember to keep breathing and allow your body to relax completely.

Now let's begin.

Start by tightening the muscles in your forehead. To do this, raise your eyebrows as high as you can. Don't strain too much. Just put in extra effort to raise your eyebrows up. Hold your eyebrows in that position for five seconds. Release them abruptly as you allow yourself to feel that tension drop.

Pause for roughly 10 seconds.

Now tense your mouth and cheeks by smiling widely. Hold for 5 roughly seconds and release. Recognize how your face feels soft.

Pause for roughly 10 seconds.

After that, move on to tense your eye muscles. Shut your eyelids as tightly as you can. Hold for roughly 5 seconds and release.

Pause for roughly 10 seconds.

Slowly pull your head to look up as though you were gazing at the ceiling. Maintain this position for about 5 seconds, then release. Feel the tension melting away from your neck muscles.

Pause for roughly 10 seconds.

Take a moment to appreciate the relaxed feeling of your head and neck.

Take a deep breath in… and breathe out.

Breathe in again, and out.

Let go of all the stress and anxiety that you might be feeling.

Breathe in and out.

Move on to clench your fists tightly without struggling too much. Hold for roughly 5 seconds. Make it count. Release.

Pause for roughly 10 seconds.

Time to flex your biceps. Tightly flex your biceps as you feel the tension building up around this muscle. Visualize your biceps tightening. Maintain this position for about 5 seconds. Release.

Take a deep breath in, and breathe out.

Next, tighten your tricep muscles. Extend your arms out and tightly lock elbows. Hold this position for about 5 seconds. Release.

Take a long deep pause for about 10 seconds. Relax.

Raise your shoulders up high as though they could touch your ears. Maintain the position for about 5 seconds. Release. Feel the heaviness of your shoulders as they drop back to their original position.

Take a long deep pause for about 10 seconds. Relax.

Now, tense your upper back. Pull your shoulders back as if you were trying to make the shoulder blades touch. Hold that position for about 5 seconds. Relax.

Take a long deep pause for about 10 seconds. Relax.

Tense your chest. Take a deep breath in… Pause for 5 seconds. Breathe out. Let go of all the tension in this area.

Gently move to your lower body and tighten your stomach muscles. Suck them in. Maintain this position for about 5 seconds. Relax.

Take a long deep pause for about 10 seconds. Relax.

Slowly arch your lower back. Hold this position for about 5 seconds. Release.

Take a long deep pause for about 10 seconds. Relax.

Pause for a moment to appreciate the sagginess of your upper body. Let go of all the tension and stress inside.

Next, tighten your buttocks. Maintain this position for 5 seconds. Relax.

Take a long deep pause for about 10 seconds. Relax.

Now, tense your thighs by pressing your knees together. Imagine holding a penny between your knees. Maintain this position for 5 seconds. Relax.

Take a long deep pause for about 10 seconds. Relax.

Tense your feet by curling your toes. Hold this position for about 5 seconds. Relax.

Take a long deep pause for about 10 seconds. Relax.

Perform a quick body scan as you acknowledge the wave of relaxation throughout your body from head to toe. Feel the lightness within you.

Breathe in... pause... breathe out.

Breathe in... pause... breathe out.

Shorter PMR Technique

Once you've mastered the PMR technique, you can quickly relax your muscles without necessarily going through all the basic procedures. This is achieved by tensing several muscle groups at a time and relaxing them. It's important that you remember to compare how your muscles feel when tense. and when relaxed. By distinguishing between relaxed and tense muscles, you will value the importance of relaxation in your body.

Let's begin. Tightly curl your fists and tense your forearms and biceps. Hold this position for about 5 seconds. Relax.

Pull your head backward as though you're gazing at the ceiling. Roll it clockwise to make a complete circle. Perform the same process anticlockwise. Relax.

Now tense your face muscles. Smile widely as you feel your cheeks tighten, Wrinkle your forehead and squint your eyes while you hunch your shoulders. Maintain this position for about 5 seconds. Relax.

Arch your shoulders back so that your shoulder blades can meet. Take a deep breath into your chest as you tighten your stomach muscles to hold this breath. Hold for about 5 seconds. Relax.

Curl your toes, tighten your thighs, calves and buttocks. Hold this position for 5 seconds. Relax.

Summary of the Muscle Groups to Tense

The following is a list of the muscle groups that you should focus on tensing while doing progressive muscle relaxation.

Muscle Group	What to Do
Forehead	Raise your eyebrows high and hold.
Bridge of the nose	Frown as much as you can.
Cheeks and jaws	Smile widely.
Eye muscles	Squint your eyelids tightly.
Neck muscles	Pull your head back as though you're looking at the ceiling.
Hands	Clench your fists.
Biceps	Tighten or flex your biceps.
Triceps	Extend your arms out and lock your elbows.
Shoulders	Lift your shoulders as if you want them to touch your ears.
Upper back	Pull your shoulders back tightly.
Chest	Take a deep breath in and hold.

Stomach muscles (Abs)	Suck your stomach muscles in.
Lower back	Arch your lower back.
Buttocks	Tighten.
Thighs	Press your knees together.
Feet	Pull your toes towards you.
Calves	Tighten your calves.
Toes	Curl your toes.

Chapter 8: Physical Meditation Techniques Guide

This section will take you through physical meditation practices as a technique that will help you relax and master calming your mind.

Meditation is a term that has been inaccurately and loosely used in the modern-day world. As a result, there is so much confusion about how to practice meditation every day. Some folks use the term meditation to refer to the everyday practice of thinking. Others misunderstand it as fantasizing or daydreaming. Meditation (Dhyana) is not anything close to these definitions.

What is Meditation?

Simply put, meditation refers to the technique of resting the mind and attaining a higher state of consciousness. Meditation is not a religion. Rather, it is a science. As such, it is a practice that sticks to a specific order and that its results can be verified (Rama, n.d.). When practicing meditation, the mind is clear and relaxed. It is inwardly focused to help in fathoming a deepened state of ourselves. During the process of meditating, you're wide awake and alert.

Nonetheless, the mind is not focused on the external world or anything that is happening around you. Instead, it focuses on your calm inner state, and this helps to quieten the mind. Once this state is achieved, nothing can distract you, and meditation deepens further.

Turning Inward

One interesting thing that you've always been taught in life is to focus on the external world. However, no school has taught us how to focus on our inner selves. The issue here is that we forget who we are and we become strangers to ourselves. The absence of self-understanding affects our lives in many ways. It is one of the main reasons why we are often disappointed in life and why most of the relationships we enter into fail to work.

Our education systems cultivate a small portion of the mind and the vast realm of unconsciousness remains undisciplined and unknown. Perhaps you might have heard that the entire body is in the mind, but the entire mind is not in the body. This phrase is true, bearing in mind that the better part of the mind remains unexploited. It is through the practice of meditation that the mind can be truly developed and controlled.

So, what is the goal of meditation? Meditation seeks to go beyond the mind and connect with our very nature - which is characterized by happiness, peace and bliss. People who meditate more often have a deeper understanding that the mind stands between ourselves and the understanding of our essential nature. It can be argued that the mind has a mind of its own, which is unruly and undisciplined. The mind will rebel against any attempts to tune it to follow a certain path. Accordingly, most people who meditate experience daydreams or fantasies. Very few people achieve the stillness that is obtained through genuine deep meditation.

Oftentimes we are taught how to adjust to the external world. We are never taught how to calm our minds and examine ourselves from within. This is what you learn through meditation. By learning how to be still and look within yourself, you gain the highest form of happiness that can be achieved by a human being. You ought to realize that all other external forms of joys are momentary. The joy of meditation is everlasting. Well, you might think that we are exaggerating things here. But it's the plain truth. The benefits of meditation are true, and they are supported by a long line of philosophers who attained the truth behind it.

You also stand to benefit from meditation, as this guide will take you through some basics of meditation. In reality, you may not become a pro from the word go. However, practice makes perfect. The more you practice how to meditate, the more you achieve a higher state of stillness that deepens your meditation practice. It's all about your commitment to the practice. Don't jump into it with excitement expecting quick results within a day. Make it a habit and you will certainly see a transformation in your life.

Guide to Cultivating Stillness

The basic idea behind meditation is that you should learn how to be still. For you to learn how to be still, you have to begin with your body before you progress to your thoughts. Traditionally, yoga required that one should be guided by a teacher to achieve the right meditation posture termed as "asana." Today, this is something that you can practice at home. By meditating regularly, you can master the art and you will find it easy to achieve the right posture to meditate.

Let's begin.

Find an uncluttered room that is quiet and where you will not be disturbed while meditating. Make yourself comfortable. Sit on a chair or the floor cushioned by a mat. Keep your back straight and gently close your eyes.

Now bring your attention to your body. Become aware of your whole body from head to toe. Relax. Release all the tension that you're feeling in your body. Let go. Meditation is all about letting go. First, let go of physical tension before you progress to your thoughts.

With your body relaxed and calm, bring your attention to your breath. Notice the areas of the body that are used as you breathe. It's important that you breathe diaphragmatically as this will help you achieve a higher state of relaxation. Continue focusing on your breath. Just notice how air is moving in and out of your body without trying to control it. You may notice that the first few moments your breath is irregular. Gradually, it gets smooth.

Your object of focus is your breath. Continue focusing on your breath in an accepting way. Don't judge, just be there to experience the beauty of breathing in and out. Open yourself fully until you feel like there is no difference between you and your breathing.

Plenty of thoughts will come to mind. You may think, "Am I doing this in the correct way?" Or "When will this end?" Or "Maybe I should have closed the door!" Or "My neck hurts." It's okay for your mind to wander.

Each thought that comes to mind will require some form of response from you, either an action, judgment, or a general interest in trailing the thought further. You may also want to lose the thought.

As you continue meditating, realize that you're only required to raise your awareness. So, become aware of how your mind is restless. Notice the thoughts that come and go without taking any action or being judgmental. You only need to be aware and let go.

Paying Attention

The science of meditation is all about attending. For instance, if you're focusing on your breath and a certain thought came to mind, you should attend to it. The point here is that you should be present to notice this thought. Accept it and it will pass. After that, you should bring your attention to your object of focus.

Usually, we tend to react to our thoughts and this is what keeps your mind busy day and night. At times you're left in a sea of confusion not knowing what to do. Meditation practice helps you to attend to whatever is happening within you without reacting. This is where all the difference comes about. Through regular meditation, you can stop your mind from incessant wandering. It is from this freedom that you will realize who you are. You will begin to realize that you're not your mind, and you will live a life full of joy and contentment.

With time, you will value the deep state of relaxation and relief that you gain from meditation. Ideally, you will have given yourself an inner vacation - an experience of a lifetime that you may have never enjoyed before.

Ordinarily, people react to experiences that come to them in the same way they react to their thoughts. For instance, if relationships do not work, people become upset. If they lose money, they become frustrated. When something negative is said about you, you become depressed. All these prove one thing: your moods/feelings are dictated by what comes before you. For that reason, you may feel as though your life is a vicious cycle of bad experiences. The problem is that you react even moments before you fully experience what you're reacting to. This is as a result of the interpretations that you have in mind about what might happen.

Your fears, resistances and prejudices limit you from enjoying life as it is. The control that you gain from meditation will help you attend to what is taking place in the present moment. Instead of reacting to things, you will understand that you're not your mind. Through acceptance, you will learn how to take on ideal responses that are most helpful to your everyday circumstances.

What Are the Signs of Progress?

You may be concerned about how you will know that you're making progress. The important thing to keep in mind is that you need to practice meditating more often for you to experience the benefits of it. Obviously, you don't plant a seed today to reap the fruits the following day. It takes time. Be gentle and patient with yourself, and practice consistently.

Top 5 Yoga Poses to Help You Relax

Statistics from the National Institute of Health shows that 9.5% of Americans do yoga exercises. As more and more people begin practicing yoga, studies reveal that many physical and mental benefits are gained by those who practice yoga. Yoga is a Sanskrit term which means the "union of the body and mind" (Tarantola, 2018). Some of the physical benefits gained from yoga include increased strength and flexibility, toning muscles, lowering blood pressure, and most importantly, encouraging relaxation. There are studies that show that yoga can also be used to alleviate back pain and arthritis, in addition to boosting mental and heart health (Tarantola, 2018).

The following are five of the best yoga poses that you can use to relax your body and mind.

Legs Up the Wall

Legs up the wall is a popular yoga pose simply because you don't have to strain yourself to assume this pose. The best part is that it can be done anywhere. It's the perfect way to unwind after a stressful day.

Find some space around you where you can lie down with your head facing away from the wall. Lift your legs up so that they can rest on the wall. For additional support, consider placing a pillow under your hips. Ensure that you're comfortable in this position for optimal relaxation benefits. You can play some soothing music to help you deepen your relaxation. Take this moment to allow your mind and body to relax. Learn to let go of any tension, thoughts, or worries may be holding on to. Make an effort to bring your mind to the present moment to achieve the calmness that you need.

Child's Pose

This is a wonderful pose that will help you relieve tension around the hips and the lower back. Start this pose by assuming a tabletop position. Slowly bring your big toes inward towards one another and widen your knees. Gently push your hips back so that your haunches are close to your heels. Now walk your hands in front of you and gradually lower your chest to the floor. Let go and relax your whole body. For extra support, consider putting a pillow under your belly. Once you've achieved the right posture, follow your breathing exercise as you release any tension from your body. Maintain this position for about 10 deep breaths. If possible, add props to modify the pose for maximum relaxation.

Forward Bend/Fold

Forward bend/fold can be done while sitting or standing. Both postures will provide you with plenty of relaxation benefits. Before assuming this position, start by taking deep breaths in and out. Do this until you notice your breath is smooth. If you want to perform this exercise while sitting down, get yourself comfortable with your legs stretched out. Next, walk your hands towards your heels as much as you can. Don't worry about touching your heels. Simply ensure that you stretch your back without straining. Lower your chest to your knees. Relax your neck and head and face forward.

If you are performing this exercise while standing, stand upright and fold yourself from this position. Move your arms to the back of your feet. Maintain this posture for 10 deep breaths.

This pose helps stimulate vital organs such as the kidneys and liver. It also improves digestion while stretching out the hamstrings, calves, and hips. Additionally, it can lower your stress levels thanks to the calming effect it has on your mind.

Corpse Pose

You might think that this is perhaps the easiest pose to assume. Well, you're wrong. Yogis argue that this is a challenging pose as most people struggle to lie there and just relax. You may notice that this pose is commonly used at the end of a yoga class. Generally, it helps to relax and calm the mind. Other potential benefits include reducing headaches, fatigue, and helping with insomnia.

Tree Pose

This is yet another awesome yoga pose for beginners. It helps to ensure that you achieve focus and clarity while standing on one foot. To practice this posture, begin by standing on both feet. After that, place your left foot on your inner right upper thigh. Put your hands together in a prayer position. Find an object in front of you to focus on, for example, you can use a candle as your object of focus.

Maintain the position for 10 breaths and switch sides. While in this position, ensure that you avoid leaning on the standing leg. It's also helpful to keep your abdominals engaged in the process.

Other Physical Meditation Techniques: Qigong

Qigong, often pronounced *chee-gun*, refers to an ancient Chinese healing exercise and technique that involves controlled breathing meditation and movement exercises (Palermo, 2015). Practicing qigong helps to ensure you maintain your Jing, bolster, and balance your Qi energy while at the same time enlightening your Shen (spirit/mind). The term "Jing" refers to your spirit (Campbell, n.d.). Qigong helps to maintain and balance your gentle spirit. Your "Qi" is your life energy, the energy that flows in all living things ("What Is Qi Energy?," n.d.)

Just like yoga, there are numerous types of qigong practiced all over the world. Some of these exercises take the form of meditation and breathing exercises to enhance spirituality and health. Others are more vivacious and they include martial arts.

Qigong and Tai Chi

Most people tend to think that qigong and tai chi are similar. However, based on the definition of both practices, they are very far from it. Tai chi, also known as tai chi chuan, is a self-paced technique of stretching and other physical exercises (Tai chi: A gentle way to fight stress, 2018). Each posture used in tai chi flows into the next posture without taking breaks. The goal is to see your body in constant motion. It's for this reason that tai chi is sometimes referred to as moving meditation. Practicing tai chi regularly has numerous health benefits for the mind, body, and spirit.

Qigong, on the other hand, is usually identified as the internal part of tai chi. Qigong exercises involve stationary movements repeated several times. "Qi" is the energy that flows in us and makes us feel alive. It's through this energy that people experience different types of emotions.

The striking difference between qigong and tai chi is that the latter involves movements that are often practiced for a specific situation. Tai chi involves full-body movements that flow in a sequence. Concepts and theories can be used in tai chi classes. Some movements of qigong can also be used in these classes, but qigong practice does not have to include tai chi.

To clearly distinguish between the two, think of a bodybuilder who strives to make their biceps bigger. In this case, the bodybuilder will build this muscle using repeated bicep curls exercises To effectively build this muscle, the bodybuilder will have to focus on that muscle only. Likewise, qigong focuses on one particular issue that one might be suffering from either physically, emotionally or spiritually. Tai chi, on the contrary, is like taking care of the whole body by exercising regularly.

You may be wondering whether you have to be physically fit for you to practice qigong or tai chi. The truth is that you don't have to be in great shape to practice either of these ancient meditation exercises. The aim of these meditation techniques is to bolster your strength, flexibility and balance.

The exciting thing about these forms of exercise is that they can be practiced anywhere and you don't require any equipment to start. When practiced correctly, tai chi and qigong can be ideal approaches to improve your overall health.

Chapter 9: Visualization Techniques Guide

Visualization, also termed as guided imagery, is a relaxation technique that uses the power of imagination to evoke positive emotions. This technique works in a simple way. You only need to picture yourself in a relaxed scene and live in the moment. It might sound too simple or too silly, but rest assured that it works. The basic idea behind visualization involves the notion of coming up with a detailed mental image of a peaceful and relaxing environment. This relaxation technique can be practiced on its own, but you can also incorporate it alongside the physical relaxation practices that we have discussed in this manual, like progressive muscle relaxation.

Why Visualization Works

You may be wondering whether visualization can really help relieve you of stress and anxiety. Guided imagery will help you relax due to a number of reasons. This technique involves a crucial element of distraction that redirects your attention away from something that might be stressing you and draws your focus towards something else. Consider visualization as a non-verbal instruction to the unconscious mind and body to act as though it was in a relaxed and calm state.

Visualization also works by bringing back good relaxation memories that will evoke pleasant sensations, which will eventually help you relax. Just like other forms of guided meditation, the goal of visualization is to help you learn how to disconnect yourself from moment to moment fixation, which often contributes to increased levels of stress and anxiety. Instead, you learn to detach yourself from thoughts and feelings and just notice them streaming through your mind and body. Practicing visualization guarantees that you improve on how you respond to stressful situations.

Here is a brief practice that you can try to have an idea of how the visualization technique works.

Think of a food that you love to eat. Really, stop for a moment and think about it. Bring the picture in mind. Close your eyes and imagine the food you thought about in front of you. Notice how amazing the food looks. Imagine its aroma and taste. Picture yourself in the present moment having the food you're thinking about.

After the brief exercise, if you were somewhat hungry, then hunger pangs must have started striking you. Perhaps your mouth is watering at the thought of the food. This example should show you the strong connection that your thoughts have with your body. Visualization leverages on this phenomenon to change how you feel.

Another example that can help you understand how visualization actually works is the effect that films can have on your emotional state. Have you ever felt depressed after watching a heartbreaking movie? Maybe the movie even left you shedding tears. This is how your thoughts can influence your moods. By mastering the power of visualization, you can use it to your advantage to influence your emotional state as you desire.

Visualization Techniques for Anxiety and Stress Reduction

The following visualization techniques should help you manage your stress and anxiety. It's strongly recommended that you use these techniques at a specified time set aside to visualize every day.

Creative Visualization of a Favorable Outcome

This type of visualization involves the idea of creating a particular outcome that you want out of a certain situation. This technique is best used when faced with a stressful situation. In this case, you should picture yourself at a time when you've solved the issue that you might be facing.

How to do it

Find a quiet place where you can make yourself comfortable. Gently close your eyes and take a deep breath. Bring your attention to the issue that is stressing you. Maybe finances have been an issue and your mind hasn't settled as a result. It could be that your marriage is not okay and it has been stressing you. Don't associate yourself with the stressful issue you may be experiencing. The key issue is to visualize the issue so that you can visualize the other side of the stressful scenario.

Now, with the issue in mind, picture yourself feeling okay after you've resolved the problem you have been facing. Imagine yourself feeling peaceful, calm, and happy that the issue has totally been resolved. Don't worry about how the matter was resolved. Visualization doesn't focus on the solutions.

Rather, it creates an image that is opposite to the negative feeling that you may be experiencing. Visualization takes your mind to a beautiful life full of joy, happiness and calmness.

It's crucial that you envisage every little detail relating to the issue you wish to resolve. What does your immediate environment look like? What are you wearing? Who are you communicating with? Remain in the visualized room and notice anything tangible. What do you see? These tangible items are helpful as they strengthen your visualization.

Most people who have successfully used visualization to manage stress agree that this exercise is effective as it brings solutions to the forefront. How does this happen? In the process of visualizing that your problem has been resolved, chances are that practical solutions to your issue might come to mind. The advantage gained here is that this lowers or expels the likelihood of feeling stressed.

Visualization as Diversion from Stress

This visualization technique can be used when you're feeling extremely stressed. The basic idea behind this technique is to imagine a peaceful scene as a means of momentary relief. The scene here can be something that you strongly desire. Visualize being in a deserted beach that you've always imagined yourself visiting, or playing with a kitten. Visualize anything that makes you relaxed and happy, and be in that moment.

How to do it

Make yourself comfortable in a quiet surrounding. Empty your mind and take a few deep breaths in and out. Now create a picture of something that would make you feel calm, relaxed, and happy.

Again, visualize all the little details that relate to the relaxation scenario that you have in mind. If you're thinking about a place, what time is it there? Is it night time or day time? Do you notice the sun shining on a body of water next to you? What are some of the sounds that you hear? What are people talking about in this beautiful place?

If you're thinking about playing with your lovely pet, what color is it? Does it have a name? What game are you playing with the pet?

The more detailed your visualization is, the better the technique will work. It draws your attention away from the mental clutter that contributed to increased stress and anxiety. This form of visualization is best used when stress mounts up or when you feel you're overly anxious. It takes practice for you to find it easy to virtually visit that beautiful place in your mind where you can relax. The good thing about this visualization exercise is that it can be practiced at any time of the day. Regardless, it makes a lot of sense for you to set some time aside to use this technique to relax and calm your mind. Remember, it's by achieving a peaceful state of mind that you'll be able to see your productivity increase and feel good about yourself and the life you live.

Visualization With Deep Breathing

Deep breathing is a powerful relaxation technique that we explored in chapter 5. Combining this technique with visualization promises outstanding results. When these techniques work together, both the mind and the body are brought to a deepened state of relaxation.

How to do it

It's recommended that you lie down to practice this technique. Start by taking a deep breath in and out. Use your breath as your object of focus. Listen to your body as you breathe in cool, fresh air into your body. Feel the warmth of the air as it escapes through your nostrils releasing tension from within.

Next, become aware of your body. Notice your body lying down and the posture that you've assumed.

Feel the contact between your body and the floor. Scan your body from the top of your head all the way down to your toes. Pay attention to all the sensations that come and go as you explore your body.

Now visualize all kinds of stress leaving your system in the form of waves through each breath. Widen your visualization. What do these waves look like? Are they colored? If so, what color are they? Which part of the body is discharging the most waves of stress?

Just like other forms of visualization, the more detailed your imagery is, the more effective your practice will be. This is a good opportunity for you to leverage your creativity and create a peaceful world in your mind where you can relax and calm your mind.

Happy Memory Visualization

There is no denying the fact that happy memories have a remarkable effect on our emotional state. Visualizing yourself being happy at a certain time is somewhat distinct from visualizations of physical things like money or your dream home. This type of visualization is highly effective as it manifests true happiness in your life. The best part is that once you learn to take your mind to these beautiful moments, you can also do the same in stressful situations.

When you're not feeling satisfied with your circumstances or with yourself, you can switch your mind to happy memories that fuel you with joy and laughter. Happy feelings will always be a useful tool to help you live a fulfilling life as these emotions strengthen the power of your thoughts. Any negative feelings that might have been hiding in your subconscious mind will automatically be eliminated. This void will be filled with positive and productive thoughts that can lead you to live a better life.

How to do it

Start by having a specific goal in mind. What do you want to achieve from this visualization? Of course, you want to imagine yourself being happy.

Select an image that is personal to you and brings back happy memories in your life. Don't be in a rush to pick an image. Take a few minutes to listen to your thoughts as you choose a memory of something that makes you truly happy. We all have that one moment that we can relate to. A time when we were genuinely happy. Choose that memory and use it for this visualization.

One thing that you should remember from the previous chapters is that practicing relaxation exercises every day is the best way of ensuring you master these techniques. Likewise, schedule your time to practice self-care through visualization. With time, your visualization will gain more clarity and you will start seeing manifestations in your life.

Let's begin.

Take a deep breath in and out. Relax and clear your mind. Pay attention to your breathing as it helps in clearing the mental jumble that is preventing you from relaxing.

Now bring your happy memory in sight. What were you wearing when this memorable occasion occurred? Who were you with? What did your friend or partner wear for the occasion? What color of clothes did you wear? Include all the fine details to strengthen your visualization.

You may fail to remember all the details, but make sure that you fill these gaps with anything that comes to mind. The important thing is to have a clear picture of this memory.

Visualize everything in your happy memory through all your five senses. Think about what you can touch, see, hear, smell or even taste. Maybe you had a wonderful meal that day. Bring your attention to all the senses to strengthen the visualized picture.

Next, take a third-person perspective of the happy scenario. Play this scene as though you were watching a movie. What was it that you did? Who were you with? What did they say or do that made you happy? Give yourself enough time to play this scene to bring back the good feelings that you felt during that day. It's all in your brain.

After that, take a first-person view of everything that happened. It's all about you and how you felt. Let the good feelings flow within you from all corners of your body. Savor the precious moment and stay there for a few minutes.

Continue playing this happy memory as you allow yourself to enjoy the experience through all your five senses. You're happy and peaceful as you can clearly remember and relate to.

Now wrap it up. You've achieved your goal of visualization. Gently let go of the image and approach the rest of the day with the renewed sense of happiness that you just felt.

Visualization for Self-Motivation

Stress can take a considerable toll on your life. It can quickly extinguish any motivation you have to do the things that you love. Individuals who are stressed often feel stagnated. Usually, you may have the feeling that things are not working out for you and this leaves you hopeless. Instead of taking action to change your life, you give up because nothing seems to work.

Visualization can turn this feeling around. Stress and anxiety fill your mind with destructive thoughts. Since your thoughts are involved here, your emotions stand to be affected, both in the short and in the long run. Visualization for self-motivation can help you regain control of your thoughts and turn the destructive thinking into positive thinking.

Ask yourself, what do you think successful people think about most of the time? Obviously, these people spend most of their time thinking about good things. They focus on what they want. That's the whole point of approaching life with optimism. You need to change your focus from thinking about what you don't want and thinking more about what you want.

So, as you use this visualization technique, know what you want and make it clear in your mind. For example, let's say you long to live in your dream home somewhere overseas, say in Australia.

Imagine yourself doing everything you can that will land you to your dream home. Reinforce your visualization by filling in all the fine details about your dream home in the location you've always wanted. Picture yourself settling down and making new friends with the locals. How do you feel about meeting new people? Imagine all the feelings that you will experience with your five senses.

It's through such visualization that you will push your mind to create ideas about how to make your dreams into a reality. At first, it may appear far-fetched. But visualization has nothing to do with knowing how you will get there. Picture yourself being in that moment and the universe will take its course.

The simplest trick behind visualization for self-motivation is to think about what you want. It's important that you develop a habit of visualizing every single day. Schedule it early in the morning and late at night moments before you go to bed.

Once the habit sticks and visualization is a non-negotiable part of your daily routine, you will find it easier to stay motivated throughout the day. The choices you make every day play a crucial part in determining how your life turns out. Therefore, if you build on your motivation to create a life that you desire every day, there is no doubt that your dreams will eventually come true.

The different visualization techniques discussed herein can be used for varying situations. Choose the best technique that suits your circumstance for the best results. For instance, when faced with a stressful situation, visualizing yourself in a happy memory can help distract your mind from negative emotions. If you're looking to get motivated as you seek to accomplish your goals, visualization for self-motivation will serve you best. The most important thing you should remember is to try your best to reinforce your visualization by adding all the little details about your mental picture. Include everything that touches on your five senses. Most importantly, visualize every single day.

Chapter 10: Combine All the Techniques in Your Daily Routine

At this point, you have learned how to practice several relaxation techniques. Maybe you've not mastered these techniques yet, but you're now aware of which techniques you should use for certain purposes. Based on experience, there are particular combinations of these relaxation strategies which creates maximum benefit to the user. This section will focus on the best blend to incorporate in your routine to reap maximum benefits from the relaxation techniques.

It's worth noting that combining two or more relaxation strategies provides you with a greater advantage simply because they create a synergistic effect. In other words, there is more to be gained by bringing together two or more techniques as compared to using one relaxation strategy alone.

Another convincing reason why you should consider combining relaxation techniques is that it helps to achieve a deepened state of relaxation as one technique builds on the calming effect of the other. Through the unique blend that we will recommend in this section, you will realize that each relaxation approach builds progressively on the preceding approach. Accordingly, there is a higher likelihood of achieving a deeper state of relaxation.

Besides, blending some of these techniques provides you with the unique benefit of saving time. You may be too busy to use one technique at a time; using two or more at a time can help you make use of the few minutes you have to perform a quick relaxation before proceeding with other important activities.

As you go through the different blends that we recommend, keep in mind that these are mere suggestions that have been proven and tested. You have the freedom to experiment with techniques that you think will serve you best. Of course, with constant practice, you will master these techniques and you will become more aware of which relaxation techniques that have a desired calming effect on you.

Fight-or-Flight Symptom Relief

The combinations presented below have been proven to be effective in relieving you of symptoms related to fight-or-flight response and stress-induced psychological issues.

Stretch and Relax

Sit comfortably on a chair and stretch your arms out. Now tighten your arms and pull them back to stretch your shoulders and chest. While doing that, tighten your legs by first curling your toes and then pulling them back to face you.

Place your right hand on your abdomen and take a deep breath in. As you breathe out, allow your hand to move with the flow of your air. Continue breathing in and out for about 10 seconds.

Gently close your eyes and start counting back from 10 to zero. Tell yourself that for every count you make, you will be more and more relaxed. Once you're through with the countdown repeat these phrases to yourself, "I am more and more peaceful and calm... I am getting more and more relaxed... I am drifting deeper and deeper into relaxation."

While in a calm state, visit your happy memory. Visualize a moment where you were totally happy and live in that moment for a few minutes. Ensure that you experience the feeling through all your senses.

When you feel that you've been in your happy memory long enough, start counting up from 1 to 10. Remind yourself that you're getting more and more alert as you finish the exercise.

I Am Grateful

There are times when you may feel like you started your day on the wrong foot. Usually, this happens when we notice that we're making mistakes in every step that we take. So, we panic and our anxiety levels go up. Our negativity bias gets the best of us and we begin feeling as though we are failures. Has this ever happened to you? You make one mistake and you feel like the world is crumbling down on you. When faced with such situations, consider using the following relaxation exercises.

Start by using the shorter version of the progressive muscle relaxation (PMR) technique we discussed in chapter 7. Curl your fists and flex your biceps. Smile widely as you wrinkle your forehead. Tense your back muscles and take a deep breath. Tense your feet by curling your toes and tightening the thighs, calves, and buttocks.

Now choose three things that have happened in your day so far that you feel grateful for. It doesn't matter whether it's a minor or major event. Choose anything that you're thankful for. It can be as simple as taking a hot shower in the morning or the breakfast that you enjoyed. It can be your colleague who helped you get to work on time or your child giving you a hug as you left for work in the morning. Take a moment or two to enjoy this experience as you relieve the stress that is slowly rising.

Continue savoring the moments that you're thankful for. Now take a first-person view of the things that you have done during the day that you are happy about. Remember, it doesn't have to be something major. Choose simple things that you did and they made your day feel worthwhile. For instance, maybe you finished a certain task on time or you helped your coworker manage something that was challenging. Stay in these positive experiences for a few minutes.

Deep Affirmation

Make yourself comfortable and take a few deep breaths in and out. While you're doing this, place your hand on your abdomen so you can notice your movements as you breathe in and out.

Gently close your eyes and perform a quick body scan from head to toe. Notice any tensions in your body. Progressively move from the top of your head as you determine whether there is any point in your body that feels tense. When you uncover a tense area, exaggerate it to raise your awareness. Tense the area where you feel some tightness, then pause for a second or two and release the tension.

Clear your mind as you strive to achieve a calm state of mind and body. Use your breathing as your object of focus to help relax your mind and clear clutter.

Now recite these affirmations with conviction.

I am happy and at peace.

Tension is draining out of my body.

I can tone down my level of tension at will.

I see peace within myself.

I am in touch with my inner peaceful self.

Relaxation is within my reach.

Note: You can edit these affirmations to suit a situation that you need to reaffirm to yourself. Maybe you're looking to make yourself feel happy or motivated. Adjust these affirmations to match that.

Once you feel relaxed long enough, stop and count from 1 to 10. Remind yourself that you're moving towards a more alert state.

Taking Control

Make yourself comfortable either on the floor or on a chair. Gently close your eyes and focus on your breathing. Notice each breath you take and the effect it has on your body. As you breathe out, imagine tension leaving your body like waves. Visualize these waves deeply. What color are these waves? Which part of your body is releasing the most waves?

Shift your attention to a situation that is making you feel stressed. Don't associate yourself with the stressful situation, just notice it. Now visualize feeling good that the situation has been resolved. Picture yourself feeling grateful that you managed to find a solution to the problem. Don't focus on the details, simply savor the good sensations flowing within you now that the problem is resolved. Remind yourself that you can handle any issue that you may be facing and be confident about it.

You can see how easy it is to combine two or more relaxation techniques. Challenge yourself to combine the techniques that work best for you. The more you practice these techniques, the better you get at it.

Set Your Goals and Manage Your Time Wisely

The relaxation techniques discussed in this manual are indeed effective and they have been proven and tested by people all over the world.

Regardless of how effective these techniques are, if you fail to incorporate them into your busy daily schedule, you might not benefit from them. This is where the issue of time comes into play. Just like hitting the gym and exercising regularly, most people will argue that they don't have time to practice these relaxation approaches every day. But guess what, you have time. The only issue that you're facing is that you have poor time management. It's for this reason that I will briefly tip you on how you can include these exercises on your everyday routine without struggling.

Set Clear Goals

Successful people have one thing in common: they have clear goals. Setting clear goals helps you to prioritize activities. The idea of setting goals doesn't necessarily mean that you should set long term goals. You can have mini-goals that you plan to accomplish before the end of the day. These mini-goals can be in the form of a to-do list. Your to-do list will help you plan your day effectively. You will be better placed to attend to the most important activities first before proceeding to do other things.

If you can complete your tasks in time, you will have a lot of spare time for other activities such as spending time with your family and friends. The few minutes or hours you create can also be used to engage in self-care.

Effective Time Management

With regards to effective time management, the following time management techniques should help you.

Eat That Frog

Mark Twain once argued that if you can eat a live frog in the morning, then you would probably go through the day with the satisfaction that there nothing worse that can happen throughout the day. The term "frog" here is used to refer to your most important task. This is the one task that you might procrastinate (Tracy, 2019). Therefore, it is advisable that you accomplish this task early in the morning before doing anything else. This time management technique can help you prioritize the most important things that you need to do. For instance, focusing on yourself should be the first thing you do right after getting out of bed.

The Pomodoro Technique

This is another remarkable time management strategy that encourages you to use the time you have instead of working against it. The idea behind this technique is that you should break your daily schedule into 25-minute chunks (pomodoros) followed by five-minute breaks. Once you complete four pomodoros, you should take a longer break of approximately 15 - 20 minutes.

The main reason why this strategy is effective is that it instills a sense of urgency in you. Instead of assuming that you have the whole day to work on something, you will understand that you only have 25 minutes to make progress. This stops you from wasting your time on distractions. Ultimately, you're more likely to have time to practice relaxation techniques.

Say "No" and Delegate

Most people go through their days feeling like they have no time because they put a lot of pressure on themselves by taking on tasks they can't handle. It's time to stop this. We all have our limits. You cannot please everyone by taking on additional tasks in your already packed schedule. Learn to say "No." This is the best thing that you can do to help yourself have some extra time to focus on yourself and practice relaxation techniques.

You should realize that there is nothing wrong with admitting that you cannot handle certain tasks. Free yourself from pressure and delegate these tasks where possible.

Develop A Positive Addiction

It's possible to develop a "positive addiction" towards feeling good, confident and competent. This is something that you can practice regularly as it depends on the outlook that you have towards life. The positive addiction that you develop will encourage you to organize yourself in a way that you complete the most important activities first. With time, you will actually be addicted to the good feeling evoked when you accomplish these tasks. To achieve this, ensure that you set small, realistic goals that are attainable.

Final Thoughts

This guide has covered all you need to know about managing stress and anxiety through relaxation techniques. Ideally, by using these techniques regularly, you will be better placed to live a happy and fulfilling life. At this point, you may have realized that there are certain things that you have been taking for granted and yet they can help you overcome stress and anxiety. Your breathing, for example, the art of breathing in and out is in itself a remedy that can ease tension in your body, mind and soul. After reading this book, you should make a deliberate effort to breathe mindfully as this can help calm your mind and bring you back to the present moment. Unfortunately, there are instances where you may find yourself skipping these relaxation techniques. The fast-paced environment that we live in can stop you from focusing on yourself. There are many things that require your attention and you can't deny the fact that things might get challenging.

However, it's important to remind yourself of the main reason why you're practicing these relaxation exercises. For instance, you want to live a happy life where you approach each day with a renewed sense of optimism. Maybe you're looking for motivation to face your everyday challenges. Life as we know it is full of ups and downs. For that reason, you need something that can remind you of your purpose for existence. In reality, connecting with your inner self is the best way in which you can truly understand who you are and your purpose in this world. Through your inner understanding, you can begin looking at life from a different perspective. You will understand that true happiness doesn't come from the external world or the material things that you have. True happiness comes from within.

Tapping into the power of your inner self is only possible through the relaxation techniques that have been discussed in this manual. Perhaps stress has been weighing down on you and it has stopped you from enjoying life. Make this book your best friend and refer to it each time you need to practice any of the relaxation exercises. You have the power to transform your life into the kind of life that you've always dreamed of. The only thing that is standing between you and your goals is your mind.

Following the bitter and tough experiences that you may have had in life, your mind might have made you believe that you cannot make it or that you're a failure. Well, guess what? These are just plain thoughts. They cannot determine your future if you learn how to control these thoughts and respond differently to them. For instance, practicing breathing exercises can shift your attention from focusing on destructive thoughts that influence how you behave. Through guided breathing meditation, you can learn how to notice your thoughts and any signs of tension in your body. You can combine this with visualization to evoke positive emotions that have a profound impact on your emotional state. At the end of the day, you will respond well without necessarily allowing stress and anxiety to get the best of you.

Conclusively, confront your excuses. Some of the excuses that you will give yourself to avoid practicing these relaxation exercises regularly are the same excuses that might have driven you to the situation you are in today. Perhaps you're a victim of procrastination. Maybe you always think that the best time to relax is when you have completed all the important tasks in your schedule. This strategy doesn't work since you may end up procrastinating in case other issues pop up. Make good use of the time management techniques pointed out in this guide. Remember, if you can manage your time well, you will manage your life well.

Good luck!

References

Buddy, T. (2016, February 2). Drinking to relieve stress may actually compound the problem. https://www.verywellmind.com/the-link-between-stress-and-alcohol-67239

Campbell, M. (n.d.). Meaning, origin and history of the name Jing. https://www.behindthename.com/name/jing

Conway, J. (2018, May 1). Plant-based foods: Consumer diet reasons U.S. 2017 L statistic. https://www.statista.com/statistics/753935/plant-based-food-diet-reasons/

Cronkleton, E. (2019). 10 breathing exercises to try: For stress, training & lung capacity. https://www.healthline.com/health/breathing-exercise#lions-breath

Destructive thinking: The hidden cause of stress. (2019, October 1). https://www.conovercompany.com/destructive-thinking-the-hidden-cause-of-stress/

Ducharme, J. (2018, May 8). A lot of Americans are more anxious than they were last year, a new poll says. https://time.com/5269371/americans-anxiety-poll/

Eat That Frog: Brian Tracy explains the truth about frogs | Brian... (2019, August 13). https://www.briantracy.com/blog/time-management/the-truth-about-frogs/

Fletcher, J. (2019). 4-7-8 breathing: How it works, benefits, and uses. https://www.medicalnewstoday.com/articles/324417

Jáuregui-Lobera, I., & Montes-Martínez, M. (2020). Emotional eating and obesity. Psychosomatic Medicine [Working Title]. doi:10.5772/intechopen.91734

Palermo, E. (2015, March 10). What is Qigong? https://www.livescience.com/38192-qigong.html

Rama, S. (n.d.). The Real Meaning of Meditation. https://yogainternational.com/article/view/the-real-meaning-of-meditation

The Recovery Village. (2020, April 7). Stress statistics. https://www.therecoveryvillage.com/mental-health/stress/related/stress-statistics/#gref

Schimelpfening, N. (2015, November 23). Why some people are more prone to depression than others. https://www.verywellmind.com/why-are-some-people-more-prone-to-depression-1067622

Selva, J. (2018). Albert Ellis' ABC model in the cognitive behavioral therapy spotlight. https://positivepsychology.com/albert-ellis-abc-model-rebt-cbt/

Star, K. (2012, January 25). How to use relaxation techniques for help with anxiety disorders. https://www.verywellmind.com/popular-relaxation-techniques-2584192

Tai chi: A gentle way to fight stress. (2018, September 26). https://www.mayoclinic.org/healthy-lifestyle/stress-management/in-depth/tai-chi/art-20045184

Tarantola, C. (2018, January 20). The proven health benefits of yoga and meditation. https://www.pharmacytimes.com/contributor/christina-tarantola/2018/01/the-surprising-ways-a-mindfulness-practice-can-improve-your-quality-of-life

Tarantola, C. (2018, January 1). The proven health benefits of yoga and meditation. https://www.pharmacytimes.com/contributor/christina-tarantola/2018/01/the-surprising-ways-a-mindfulness-practice-can-improve-your-quality-of-life

What Is Qi Energy? (n.d.). https://www.qienergyexercises.com/what-is-qi-energy.htm

www.ingramcontent.com/pod-product-compliance
Lightning Source LLC
Chambersburg PA
CBHW071953070526
44583CB00015B/1174